Five Minutes with the Holy Spirit

GETTING TO KNOW THE BEST
FRIEND IN THE WORLD

Ed Citronnelli

TRILOGY CHRISTIAN PUBLISHERS
Tustin, CA

Trilogy Christian Publishers
A Wholly Owned Subsidiary of Trinity Broadcasting Network
2442 Michelle Drive
Tustin, CA 92780

Five Minutes with the Holy Spirit

Copyright © 2024 by Ed Citronnelli

Scripture quotations marked (KJV) taken from The Holy Bible, King James Version. Cambridge Edition: 1769.

Scripture quotations marked NKJV are taken from the New King James Version®. Copyright © 1982 by Thomas Nelson. Used by permission. All rights reserved.

All rights reserved, including the right to reproduce this book or portions thereof in any form whatsoever.

For information, address Trilogy Christian Publishing

Rights Department, 2442 Michelle Drive, Tustin, CA 92780.

Trilogy Christian Publishing/ TBN and colophon are trademarks of Trinity Broadcasting Network.

For information about special discounts for bulk purchases, please contact Trilogy Christian Publishing.

Trilogy Disclaimer: The views and content expressed in this book are those of the author and may not necessarily reflect the views and doctrine of Trilogy Christian Publishing or the Trinity Broadcasting Network.

10 9 8 7 6 5 4 3 2 1

Library of Congress Cataloging-in-Publication Data is available.

ISBN 979-8-89041-939-2

ISBN 979-8-89041-940-8 (ebook)

Dedication

With honor, love, and gratitude, I dedicate this book to my best friend, the Holy Spirit. I remember when I first met You. Your sweet, gentle, and tender Presence started me on a journey that no other person could match. You have been with me all these years, teaching me, helping me, leading me, and guiding me. We have prayed together, traveled together, cried together, and spent time alone together in our favorite place, my little prayer room. There, I have learned Your ways, felt Your heartbeat, and been taught by You. It has been in our intimate times alone that I have come to know who You really are. At first, I heard of You, many times I preached of You, at times I witnessed Your power and felt Your Presence. But one day my preaching of You will end, and my being with You for all eternity will begin. On that day, I will see You face to face. I love You, my Friend and dearest companion. With this book, I honor You. Thank You for everything.

—Ed Citronnelli

Dedication

Contents

Dedication iii

Preface vii

Chapter 1: "Five More Minutes, Five More Minutes" 1

Chapter 2: How Did I Get Up Here? 5

Chapter 3: Holy Spirit, I Want to Know You 9

Chapter 4: Baseball and the Heights 11

Chapter 5: My First Supernatural Experience with the
    Supernatural 16

Chapter 6: The Day the Lord Jesus Appeared to Me 19

Chapter 7: The Day I Saw His Power for the First
    Time 22

Chapter 8: Backslidden, Again 25

Chapter 9: When the Power Came (How I God Filled
    with the Holy Ghost) 30

Chapter 10: "Pick It Up and Call" 36

Chapter 11: Dreams, Dreams, and More Dreams 39

Chapter 12: Satan Made the Bride Cry 42

Chapter 13: Lucifer Walks into My Room 46

Chapter 14: The Day Everything Changed 51

Chapter 15: "Follow Him" 56

Chapter 16: The Secret Place of Power 60

Chapter 17: First the Spirit, Then the Voice 67

Chapter 18: The Secret to Your Success 71

Chapter 19: Knowing His Voice 77

Chapter 20: Recognizing When He Moves (He Will
    Guide You) 82

Chapter 21: Ambassador of the Spirit 86

Chapter 22: From Washington Heights to the Ends
    of the Earth 90

About the Author 94

Preface

Many great men and women of God have written books on the ministry of the Holy Spirit. These books have been of great help to those of us in the Body of Christ. I did not want to write another book on what the Holy Spirit can do. The works of the Holy Spirit are so vast that, if written, every one, I suppose that even the world itself could not contain the books that should be written. The passion that burns in the deep chambers of my soul is for the Holy Spirit to be known by everyone as a Person and a Friend—a Person who is powerful yet gentle. He is a Person who leaps with joy yet can be grieved, one that is humble yet full of authority, and one that has feelings like you and I because He is a Person; in fact, this person is God Himself, and He is my Best Friend.

Today, the Church has forgotten the importance of who He really is and His role among the people of God. In many churches, the Holy Spirit is non-existent. At best, many have reduced Him to a proverb or a program. Some are even saying that He is not for today. Many do not believe that He is in the world today.

One day, as I was in a region called Nagaland, in the country of India, for some gospel meetings, a man came to the house where I was staying. He came to invite me to be the speaker for the following year's revival meetings. This man was very influential in his government and among his people. God had put a passion in his heart for the Holy Spirit to be poured out once again among the churches there. It was in 1976 when the last revival fire broke out in Nagaland. Since that time, the churches in that region had not been visited with the glory of the Spirit of God. Some churches were spiritually dry, and this man was desperate. God had spoken to him about His desire to pour out His Spirit once again there. Within the ranks of some influential leaders of the churches, Satan's lies were being perpetrated and believed, saying that the Holy Spirit was not something to be believed in anymore. They were saying that there was no Holy Spirit today. Remember, this was the same region where, in 1976, the Holy Spirit had come down with fire, and a great revival had broken out among them. Satan's lies have worked in extinguishing the fire of the Spirit among these wonderful people. This man is still in pursuit of the visitation of the Holy Spirit among his people. I pray that God will open the hearts of the church leaders there.

Today, this satanic scheme is still going on in many churches where Jesus' name is called upon. What a tragedy!

In view of the practicality of this subject today, I did not want to write a book on pneumatology, which is the doctrine or theology of the Holy Spirit, for this would have been too technical and too "heady," informing the mind only, and not moving the soul. Let us give that responsibility to the schools and seminaries of theology instead. They know better than I do how to do that. But I wanted to write simply about a Person that I met a few years ago that changed my theology and my life. This Person is clearly written about in the pages of the Bible, which millions read, yet so few know Him as a Person and thus as a Friend.

As you read this book, you will read not only about what He has done in the past, but also what He can do for you today, and what He will do in the future. Most importantly, I want to share with you about who He really is. You will discover that this Person called the Holy Spirit does not respond to His name as much as He responds to the name of Jesus Christ. Yes, we will speak about His power. Still, I will share about His character, His heart, and personality, which are far better. Yes, I will speak about His ministry, but most importantly, I will speak to you about how much He wants to be your close Friend. I will take you through my journey with Him. You will laugh and cry with me. You will have access to my prayer room, and there hear our most intimate conversations.

As the book develops, I pray that you will begin to see the beautiful smile on the face of this wonderful Person. I wish that each word would get your heart beating more substantially and faster for His Presence. It is my prayer that as the chapters progress, your soul will become thirsty like a deer panting for water and that a new fire will kindle on the altar of your heart for Him. To hear about Him is to desire His company; to read about Him is to wonder who He is. But to be with, to walk with, and to spend your time with Him is to know the greatest Person in the world. Come and meet my Best Friend, the Holy Spirit.

CHAPTER 1

"Five More Minutes, Five More Minutes"

It was the springtime of 2012. The winter snow had melted away, and the sun started to break through again as I prayed early in the morning in my prayer room before going to work. After kneeling at my altar with my eyes closed, I knew He was there. I knew that this Person I had become close with had come to meet me. And each day, He did. The time we spent together was full of glory. We would talk, I would cry, and His Presence would envelop me in ecstasy. In those days, I found a Person, a Friend that I could come to be with. He was never tired. He was never angry or in a bad mood. He knew my troubles and the deepest secrets of my heart. He was always welcoming. Patiently, He always took the time to answer anything I asked Him.

I could talk to Him about everything in my heart. I could share my secrets, fears, and every mistake without being judged by Him. The moment He would come, His Presence melted my heart. Tears of gladness, love, and joy would immediately roll down my cheeks. I couldn't help it. Sometimes I would say to myself, "I'm not going to cry, I'm not going to cry," but to no avail. I would start weeping right away. His Presence and love melted me each time. I felt He longed for me to be with Him every morning. Every time I entered that prayer room, it seemed that the room would be transformed, the atmosphere would change, and time would be suspended. Once I sensed His Presence, I wanted to stay with Him. Outside the window, a faint light would try to enter through the royal blue curtain covering it. I could hear my wife's and children's footsteps above the prayer room. Were they aware of where I was? I was lost in heaven. I was lost in Him. Oh, how I loved His Presence. It meant everything to me. From the first day I met Him, I fell in love with His Presence and love for me. His gentleness, kindness, patience, longsuffering, and love drew me to Him. After two or three hours of prayer and being with my Best Friend, it was getting late; it was time for me to go to my office. I got up from my knees and headed to the door of the room. As I approached to open the door to leave, I heard a voice behind me coming from the altar area of the room. The voice filled the room. It was tender, gentle, warm, and full of love. Almost hesitant but strongly longing for companionship, it said, "Five more minutes, five more minutes." I stopped at the door before I could open it. My heart melted, and I turned around and began to cry. I went back on my knees in front of the altar, weeping.

I was sobbing like a baby. My tears were tears of gratitude, joy, gladness, and brokenness. How can God, the most powerful being in the universe, have so much love for me, a frail human being? What happened broke me and humbled me. I could not understand it. All I kept saying was, "Oh Lord, oh Lord! Why do You care and want to spend time with me?" I was weeping and weeping. His Presence intensified inside the room. I was caught up in His heart, and He was in mine. We became one. He in me, and I in Him.

That day, I understood more than ever that God the Father, Son, and Holy Spirit desire to spend more time with you than they do with the angels in heaven. How can I know that? Simple, because I experienced it that day in my prayer room. How can I know that? Because of the Cross. The Cross is the most significant symbol of love that the world will ever know. It is the voice of God calling the entire world to Himself. Scripture tells us, *"Greater love has no one than this than to lay down one's life for his friends"* (John 15:13 NKJV). It was at the Cross that God, in the form of a man, gave His life for you and me. Sin separated us from God, but the Cross brought us back together again. Want more proof? Not only did Jesus willingly lay down His life for us and was raised from the dead, but also, we have His Holy Spirit available to us today. All by the will of the Father. Beloved, the Cross is God's heart exposed to the world. His love for us makes Him long for our time and companionship. His love for us is why the Holy Spirit told me that day, "Five more minutes, stay five more minutes." You can be with any human being, be it your spouse, children, friends, family members, or anyone, and all will satisfy a portion of your heart. But to be asked for, longed for, and to spend time with the Holy Spirit is like none other. His very Presence will fill your heart to a depth only He knows how to fill. That day, hearing Him say those words changed my life. It will change yours, too, as you hear Him say those exact words to you. Get ready to know love and companionship like you have never seen before. I want to share with you a Person that changed my life, He who is all-powerful, yet sensitive, gentle, and loving. He wants to spend time with you. I want you to know Him like He wants to be known. Peter, James, John, the rest of the disciples, and the prophets in the Bible knew Him. He wants to have fellowship with you if you are ready to meet Him and walk with Him. You and He will become Best Friends. You will know His thoughts, and He will know yours. You will share secrets that only you two will know of each other. When you meet Him like I did that Spring morning in 2012, you will meet the Best Friend in the world!

"The grace of the Lord Jesus Christ, and the love of God, and the fellowship of the Holy Spirit, be with you all. Amen." (2 Corinthians 13:14 NKJV)

CHAPTER 2

How Did I Get Up Here?

"No one can come to Me unless the Father who sent Me draws him."

(John 6:44 NKJV)

My first experience with my Best Friend, the Holy Spirit, happened in a little Baptist church in Ranger, Texas, in October 1983, during my first year in college. My roommate, Ryan[1], also from New York, was a pitcher on the baseball team and an ardent Christian on campus. Every week, he would invite many of the baseball players on the team to the church he attended. None of us were interested. We were baseball players, and we were in college — we didn't want to "waste time" going to church. We were consumed with the game. Our focus was on playing baseball and doing well enough to get drafted by a major league team and become major league baseball players one day. There was no time for going to church!

Well, one day, after many tries and many rejections, Ryan tried once again to invite us to the Tuesday night church service

---
1 Several names in this book have been changed.

that he religiously attended at a small church in town. This time, however, a few of us decided that to get him to stop asking, we would accept Ryan's invitation. "Let's just go to church with him this once," we told ourselves. "This way, he will leave us alone." So, that Tuesday night, a group of about twelve of us went to the small Baptist church in Ranger, Texas, where our college was. We were a less-than-captive audience. We all sat in the back, half asleep and waiting for the preacher to finish his sermon so we could get back to reality – college and baseball.

"How Did I Get Up Here?"

Toward the end of the service, the small Mexican-American preacher Brother Chuck finished his sermon and made an altar call. "Every eye closed and every head bowed, please," he said. "If anyone here wants to come up and receive Jesus Christ as their Savior, please come now, and I will pray with you."

Well, none of us wanted Jesus, so none of us got up to go forward for the prayer. All we wanted was baseball. As I was sitting in my seat with my eyes closed, thinking about how I was NOT going up there, I suddenly heard a voice say to me, "Open your eyes." I opened my eyes to a strange thing. To my surprise, I found myself standing in front of the preacher and having no idea how I got there. "Brother, do you want to receive Jesus Christ as your Lord and Savior?" the preacher asked as I stood with him before the church. I looked at him and where I had been sitting just a few seconds ago. "How did I get up here?" I asked myself. I was baffled. Over and over, I muttered the question. "How did I get up here?" One moment, I was sitting down, saying that I wasn't going to go up there, and the next moment, I found myself 50 feet away and where I said I wasn't going. "I was sitting in the back of the church!" I exclaimed.

From the back of the church to the front was quite a distance; to this day, I don't remember getting up from my seat and walking up to the altar. "How did I get up here?" I sounded like a broken record to myself. "This has never happened to me," I continued. I was dumbfounded. He asked me again, "Brother, do you want to give your life to Jesus?" At this point, I was experiencing a strange thing about this Jesus I had never experienced before. "How did I get up here?" I said to myself again. I looked at the preacher. He didn't know what had just happened to me. He looked at me, and I looked at him, confused. He asked me again, "Brother, would you like to —" I didn't let him finish the sentence. "Yes," I said. He led me through the Sinner's Prayer. I accepted, received, and believed the prayer. Then he said, "Brother, congratulations! Welcome to Jesus Christ." I looked around, and about seven other baseball players had also come up after me to receive Jesus Christ as Savior. Immediately, the Pastor announced that there would be a baptism service the following Sunday for those who had been saved that night.

After the service, we went back to the college campus. Again and again, the broken record played in my mind, "How did I get up there?" The whole night, I was not able to sleep. I kept trying to figure out how I got to the front of the church without realizing it. Later, as I grew in the Lord, I understood that the Holy Spirit had supernaturally transported me there. I had an experience like Ezekiel had so many times (Ezekiel 37:1), and like Philip had when the same Holy Spirit transported him from a river in Gaza to Azotus — a city twelve miles away — after he had baptized the Ethiopian eunuch (Acts 8:39-40). This experience is called transportation and not translation. Transportation is when the Holy Spirit carries a person physically from one place to another, and translation is when He takes a person spiritually from one place to another. Remember, witches, warlocks, sorcerers, voodoo workers, juju priests, and many other satanic agents practice this, but they do it by demonic power. It is incredible how Satan likes to imitate everything the Holy Spirit does.

CHAPTER 3

Holy Spirit, I Want to Know You

"Lord Jesus, I want more of You. Lord, touch me afresh. Oh God, I'm so hungry for Your Presence. Holy Spirit, I want to know You like other men of God have known You— like my spiritual father Bishop Bryant knows You, like Benny Hinn knows You, like Kathryn Kuhlman, Smith Wigglesworth, and the Apostle Paul knew you. Oh God...."

Tears filled my eyes and ran down my cheeks as I said the words above. I was alone in my prayer room, where I spent much time alone with the One that had become my Best Friend. I would stay in that room until I sensed His Presence. The atmosphere would immediately change. Without even consciously wanting to, I could not stop tears from rolling down my face. It was the time I was waiting for—the reason for wanting to be there. The time had come, and with it His Presence! His Person entering the room changed everything. It felt like time was suspended. I was caught in a place where there is total peace and love. Joy and ecstasy took over the atmosphere of my heart.

I could not stop crying. In my head I didn't want to cry, but my heart melted with His fragrance. At the time and still today, my greatest desire is the koinonia of the Holy Spirit. This Greek word is often translated as fellowship, but it means so much more. Koinonia is deep and mutual. It is an intercourse of thoughts, ideas, and desires. All parties involved have to put something into it. Koinonia is not the fellowship itself but rather the fruit of fellowship. Please understand that time alone with the Holy Spirit is one of my sincerest longings and greatest joys since the day I met Him. My habit of being alone with Him started immediately. I would get up early in the morning to seek Him. The house would be quiet. I would sneak out of bed, leaving my wife sleeping. I would go to my prayer room excited to meet Someone I longed to be with. The more I spent time with Him, the more I wanted to know Him. I would spend hours in His Presence longing to know more of who He was, wanting to hear His heartbeat, know His mind, and be with Him. I wanted to be more with Him than with my wife and children. All these years later, I still have those same desires to know Him more and more. His companionship means everything to me. He is the best Friend I've ever known. He has changed my life, and all that I am today is because of Him. I want you to know Him like I desire to know Him. If you sincerely desire to know Him, He will make Himself known to you, and your life will be changed forever. Get ready to go on the most remarkable journey you will ever be on—a trip of a lifetime. Get ready to meet - THE BEST FRIEND IN THE WORLD!

CHAPTER 4

Baseball and the Heights

I was born in 1964 to Dominican parents in the Dominican Republic during the reign of a dictator named Trujillo. When I was little, my mother emigrated to the United States. After some time, my brother, Alexis, and two of my sisters, Carmen Julia and Lourdes, followed. When we first arrived, we lived in Lawrence, Massachusetts, before moving to New York City in 1975. We lived in several neighborhoods but then settled in the Washington Heights area of New York in 1976.

When I was growing up there, the Washington Heights neighborhood in New York City was home to many different ethnic groups. The Irish, the Jews, the Italians, the Puerto Ricans, and, of course, the Dominicans all called Washington Heights home. All the kids in the neighborhood practically grew up together. It was a melting pot, but still our little Dominican Republic. Everything you could find in our native land you could find in our neighborhood. The typical Spanish food, the music, the language, the Dominican traditions, everything was there. The community felt like one giant extended family. All the kids attended the same schools, and everybody knew everybody. We were there to stay, and we loved it! Our families never moved from the neighborhood. Besides, for financial reasons, nobody could afford to move out anyway.

As we were growing up, many of us kids had different interests, but we all loved baseball. It is not surprising. Every Dominican kid loves baseball! Around the neighborhood, they used to say that every Dominican boy is born with a baseball bat in his hands and that béisbol (Spanish for baseball) is his first word. They would say that every Dominican boy dreams of playing in the Big Leagues one day. And this was also my desire.

Some of my neighborhood friends took the wrong road. They dropped out of school and thus had no education. Some turned to the streets to sell drugs, causing some to wind up dead and others to end up in jail. Not so for me. I was busy playing baseball. Today, I believe that God had a predestined plan for my life. He chose me in Himself before the foundation of the world (Ephesians 1:4), and because of this, I believe He used baseball to keep me out of trouble. Not only that, but He also used the game of baseball to bring me out of Washington Heights and give me a free college education.

Falling In Love With The Game

I didn't play baseball until my family and I moved to Washington Heights. As we settled into the neighborhood and I saw the other kids playing stickball on the street, I immediately wanted to join the game. They always appeared to be having so much fun. But I was the new kid on the block, and no one knew me. It took two or three months before the other kids invited me to play with them. As I started participating in the games, I quickly noticed that my baseball skills needed to be better than theirs. They were only 10 or 12 years old but had played much longer than I had. They looked so advanced that I was almost afraid to play in the games that they would organize. But as I met them and began to play among them, we quickly became friends. There was one we called "Mad Dog," because when he played, he would be so aggressive that he looked mad. There was "Choco," who according to him, loved chocolate so much. There was Hil, Mad Dog's brother. There were Rob, Jackson, Kiko, and a guy named Niño. There were "Yeco" and June. There were so many others, too, who we grew up with, but this was the leading group who would always get together to play. We all became very close friends. I am still friends with all of them to this day.

I became a better player as I continued playing and learning the game. The better I became, the more I was asked to play, and soon, they began to ask me to play all the time. I grew stronger and developed into one of the best baseball players, not only on our block but also in the organized youth leagues that we would play in during the summer months. The coaches of the organized clubs loved having me. As my reputation for baseball grew, doors began to open for me to travel outside of Washington Heights. I played baseball in the Bronx leagues and Brooklyn with a well-known team at the time called Youth Service League. The coach, Mike, was very well known in baseball because many of his players went on to play at the college level or signed contracts to play professionally. Some of his players even made it to the major leagues.

God Likes Baseball, Too

By the grace of God, I went away to college in Texas for two years to play baseball on an athletic scholarship. During my first year in college, the Los Angeles Dodgers chose me in the third round of the 1984 Winter Professional Baseball Draft. However, I turned down the offer to continue my college education. During that same year, I met Jesus Christ personally and supernaturally and gave my life to Him. At the end of two years in Texas, I transferred to the University of Louisiana to pursue baseball and my education. Still, by this time, Jesus was already moving inside my heart.

God used Baseball to get me out of harm's way and out of Washington Heights, New York, but now I understand this was a means to an end. I played at the top college level and then chose to play professionally, but baseball was not God's plan for me. His perfect plan was for me to step into the ministry and eventually preach the Gospel of His Son, Jesus Christ, worldwide. I didn't know God liked baseball! Yet, He used baseball and my love for it as an instrument for His glory and to draw me to Himself.

Baseball Hall Of Fame

After my last year at the University of Louisiana, I signed a professional baseball contract with a team called the Salt Lake City Trappers in Utah. "This is what I am alive for. I've waited for this all my life," I said. I was sure I was on my way to the Big Leagues. Though this was a minor league baseball team, it was owned by major league money. During my summer playing with the Trappers, God liked baseball. He went with me to every at-bat and every time I took the field. I had a very successful first year in my professional baseball career. I was in the top three in the league for home runs, runs batted in, and, well — I'm not proud of this — STRIKEOUTS!

Even so, during my summer playing with the Trappers, our team established a new professional winning streak record, which still stands as of the writing of this book. We won 29 consecutive games, breaking a professional baseball record that had stood for almost 100 years. We also won the league championship. All the players on the team were excited, me included. We were on our way to stardom and became a national sensation overnight. We were on the television news almost daily. We were in the newspapers. We were in sports magazines and interviewed on radio talk shows. We got national attention, and we loved it.

Because of the winning streak, our team's picture, the record-breaking ball, the game jersey, and one of our bats were taken to the Professional Baseball Hall of Fame in Cooperstown, New York. Wow! How many people pick up a baseball and aspire to play professionally? How many major league players play their entire careers and never make it to the Hall of Fame? Well, without ever making it to the Big Leagues, the members of my team and I made it that year into the Baseball Hall of Fame. You can see for yourself! Our team picture is there, and I'm right in it. What a mighty God we serve! I told you God likes baseball.

> *"For I know the thoughts that I think toward you says the Lord, thoughts of peace and not of evil, to give you a future and a hope."* (Jeremiah 29:11 NKJV)

CHAPTER 5

My First Experience with the Supernatural

"There shall not be found among you anyone that maketh his son or his daughter to pass through the fire, or that useth divination, or an observer of times, or an enchanter, or a witch, Or a charmer, or a consulter with familiar spirits, or a wizard, or a necromancer. For all that do these things are an abomination unto the Lord."

(Deuteronomy 18:10-12a KJV)

It was 11:23 p.m. I was just a kid at the time, only 12 or 13 years old, but I still remember looking at the clock to see what time it was. I was awakened by the sound of music and people talking in the living room of my house, and for some reason, I had to know what was going on out there. I got out of bed and walked to the door of my bedroom. Quietly, I crept down the hall towards the living room. I knew I couldn't be seen or heard out of bed if I wanted to know what was happening.

As I walked carefully down the hallway, I finally reached a place where I could not be seen but could look inside the living room. Just like I have remembered the time all these years, to this day, I haven't forgotten what I witnessed in the living room that night. It was strange and, at the time, frightening. Yet, I didn't turn away or leave. I heard people speaking to a woman who supposedly had the answer to human life. Only, when she spoke, she didn't have the voice of any woman I had ever heard. This voice barely sounded human. It was grotesque and deep. It sounded like a strange man or some weird being. What made it even more interesting was that I recognized the woman talking! She was my older brother's girlfriend at the time. She always visited us on Friday nights, but my brother wasn't home that night.

Exposed To The Spirit World

As I watched the scene unfold, I noticed a specific type of Spanish music playing and that the music was rendering homage to a particular name. A few years later, I discovered that the name in this music is the name of a demon considered a god in the Santeria religion. As the music played, I saw a family member put some rum inside her mouth and then spew it out, spraying it on the face of the demon-possessed woman. She would also blow smoke from a cigar into her face. As this was done, the other adults in the room began chanting. Suddenly, the woman entered a frenzy and began convulsing on the floor. She was rolling everywhere. She was foaming at the mouth and grinding her teeth. When this happened, about five men who were present got up and went about trying to control her. The young woman only weighed about 115 pounds, but her power was more substantial than theirs. I was afraid as I hid and watched this, but I couldn't look away.

Suddenly, a man's voice began to speak clearly through my brother's girlfriend. Her eyes changed and became coldly dark. It certainly was no longer her. This entity had taken control of this young woman's faculties and was not of this world. It spoke in a human language but was not human; this was a demon spirit. I watched as it began foretelling some people's futures in the room. They were worshipping this demon as a god and knew its name. Among the Latino community, witchcraft, Santeria, Voodoo, Spiritism, Macumba, Palo Mayombe, and the like are prevalent. I didn't know it then, but the demon I watched speak through my brother's girlfriend that night was a spirit of the seven African powers worshiped in Santeria.

All in one night, this was my introduction to the supernatural world — seeing my family dabble in occult practices in my living room. What I witnessed that night left a mark on my life forever. It opened my eyes and my understanding of the reality that there is a world beyond the one we see and that the inhabitants of that world are not natural but supernatural. Little did I know then that God had another life-changing collision with the spiritual realm planned for me. I couldn't have fathomed then that years later, God would introduce me to the best Friend in the world — the Holy Spirit — and call me to fight against the same evil, supernatural forces once being worshiped in my living room. I couldn't have known that the Lord, through the empowerment and instruction of the Holy Spirit, would use me one day to cast the powers of darkness out of people so that they could be free and live an abundant life like Jesus said. I couldn't have known that one day, with just the authority of His name, He would use me to subdue the wickedness that five men couldn't hold down in my living room.

CHAPTER 6

The Day the Lord Jesus Appeared to Me

Then He said, "Hear now My words: If there is a prophet among you, I, the Lord, make Myself known to him in a vision; I speak to him in a dream."
(Numbers 12:6 NKJV)

During my years serving the Lord Jesus, heaven has privileged and graced me to have Him appear in my dreams. One such time, which had a tremendous impact on my life, took place a few days after my conversion. I didn't know it then, but this dream and many of the ones that followed were the beginning of the Lord preparing my spirit for ministry. On this occasion, the Lord Jesus Christ and Satan appeared to me. The Lord Jesus was standing on my left side at a distance, while Satan was standing to my right, also at a distance. Jesus was wearing a long white robe. He had shoulder-length brownish hair, but I could not see His face.

On the other hand, Satan was standing in darkness and trying to persuade me with his words. As I stood between them,

Satan spoke and tried to sway me toward his side. While he was talking, I looked to my left where the Lord Jesus was standing, but Jesus was not saying a word. It was as if He was letting me make my own choice — He was allowing me to choose between Satan and Himself.

In the meantime, Satan continued trying to get me to choose him. His words were very influential and full of flattery. Each time he said something, and I listened, I would be drawn closer to him. When I paid attention to his words, I would find myself inching closer and closer to his side. Soon enough, I was standing just a few inches away from him. One more word, and I would be entirely on the side of Satan. To this day, I do not remember what he said, but as he said one last thing, I was drawn to him almost totally. I remember realizing I did not want him and shouted, "NOOOOOOO!" At this, a force I could not see shot me over to where Jesus was standing, and I awoke out of the dream.

As a young believer, I realized through this dream that there is a conflict between God and Satan and that we are the prize in the middle. When you read about the serpent and Eve in Genesis, you conclude that this conflict began in history. Remember how the serpent enticed Eve with his words in the Garden of Eden? I experienced the forceful and pressured words of Satan for enticement. I encourage you to be careful about which words you give your attention to. The words you open your ears to will eventually reach your heart. Words carry power. God used His Word to create the universe and the earth. But He also used His Word to curse different nations and people. Words can kill and destroy, as well as build and encourage. Jesus said,

"Take heed what you hear. With the same measure you use, it will be measured to you; and to you who hear, more will be given." (Mark 4:24 NKJV)

Satan understands the power of words. He uses your word against you as his number one tool to carry out his deceptions and mislead people into error. We must measure with the Word of God everything that comes into our ears. If what you hear contradicts God's Word, discard it, reject it, and dismiss it from your life.

CHAPTER 7

The Day I Saw His Power for the First Time

As mentioned previously, after college, I signed a contract and began playing professional baseball in the minor leagues. When that baseball season ended in Salt Lake City, Utah, I moved back to New York City. Once back in the city, I began to go about my business in my personal life and forgot about God. Of course, I wasn't drinking, doing drugs, or womanizing, but a life without God is empty and void, regardless. In 1988, I married my wife Carol, a Roman Catholic. I was not walking with God in any way, so I was neither Roman nor Catholic, nor Christian, nor anything but a backslider.

One day, while walking in the Wall Street area in Manhattan looking for a job, I came across my friend Ryan. Yes! My college roommate, Ryan — the same person God had used to bring me to Christ in Texas! We started talking, and I told him that since moving back to New York three years prior, I had stopped going to church and was not walking with the Lord Jesus. His response? He invited me to a church he was attending in

Brooklyn, New York. I took the invitation and went to service the following Sunday. It was a powerful church. This church was different from what I had seen in the small Baptist church in Texas. There was a power that the pastor moved by. It was so tangible, so real. It caught my attention. As I was sitting in the back of the church with Ryan, the pastor asked for everyone to stand. As we stood, he began to prophesy and tell people about their situations and future. I stood there with my eyes closed and began to pray, asking the Lord to speak to me through this man. Suddenly, the pastor looked toward where I stood and said, "Brother Ryan, bring that young man next to you up here; he was just asking God to speak to him." When I heard that, I opened my eyes. My heart started to pound, and my knees became weak. It was true! I had just finished asking God that. I was shocked. A fear of the Presence of God came upon me. This man's eyesight was failing him, from what I heard later. Accordingly, there was no way that he could have seen me at that distance with his natural failing eye vision. Ryan brought me to the front, and the pastor began to prophesy over me. I didn't know what a prophecy was, but I felt a Presence I had not felt before in any church. He started to speak about my future. As he laid his hands on me, I felt a power like no other I had ever experienced. It was as if God Himself was talking to me. I don't remember much of what he said concerning my future; I was so overwhelmed. But I remember that he mentioned God's glory would be upon me. Wow!

It was the first time God had spoken to me in this way. At the time, I didn't even know that God spoke to people through other people. It was a powerful church. That day, I saw healings, prophecies, and people being set free from demon spirits. I saw the Holy Spirit's power in action for the first time.

He's Forgotten In The Church Today

Today, it saddens me to see that many have forgotten that the power of the Spirit brought people to believe in Jesus in the Book of Acts. It was the Holy Spirit's power working mighty signs and wonders through the hands of the apostles that added believers to the church. The Book of Acts clearly states,

> *"And by the hands of the apostles were many signs and wonders wrought among the people.... And believers were the more added to the Lord, multitudes both of men and women."* (Acts 5:12,14 NKJV)

You, my friend who is reading this book — whether you have been called to minister the Gospel of Christ to the lost person in business, in government, or on a college campus — need the power of the Holy Spirit. No matter who you are or what you are called to do, whether you are a minister, a leader, or a simple believer, it would help if you operated in the power of the Holy Spirit. He was the key to the success of Jesus while He was on earth. The Spirit of God was also the success of the apostles and prophets in the Bible and is the key to your success. Herein is the secret to success in this world.

CHAPTER 8

Backslidden, Again

"This poor man cried out, and the Lord heard him, and saved him out of all his troubles."

(Psalms 34:6 NKJV)

"You have ruined this man's reputation and smeared his name. I wish this man would sue you for everything you have." These were the words of a judge to the Assistant District Attorney in New York City in June 1995. The City of New York had falsely accused me, though the court system eventually dropped the charges. The Bible clearly says that "all things work together for good to them that love God, and to them who are the called according to His purpose." (Romans 8:28 NKJV) Though the District Attorney tried to make a case, the American justice system prevailed in finding someone — me — innocent until proven guilty.

Since baseball didn't work out, I eventually became a police officer in the City of New York. I wanted more than just any old nine-to-five job. I wanted to do something exciting! I was looking for my destiny, not knowing that God had already laid it out for me before I was born. While working in the Police Department, I was wrongly accused because of my association with a long-time childhood friend. We had grown up in the same neighborhood of Washington Heights, but he was a drug dealer and I was a police officer. The two don't mix.

One day, he called me, asking if I could inquire about a vehicle of his that the Police Department had impounded. Because he was a childhood friend, I thought there was no harm in doing this. I made phone calls within the department to identify the vehicle's whereabouts. I was helping him find the location of the impound where the car had been taken so that he could pay the necessary fees and retrieve his vehicle. Unbeknownst to me, the car had been impounded because another police officer had found drugs inside the vehicle. When I made the phone call and identified as a police officer, the investigators suspected I was involved in suspicious activities. Based on this assumption, I began to be questioned. I had never gotten involved with drugs or alcohol. Still, in Washington Heights, as in many other New York City neighborhoods, it was not unusual for some kids to get involved in dealing with drugs. Thankfully, God had used baseball to get me away from that. As a child, even though I grew up amid it, I never took or dealt with drugs or alcohol. I never even smoked—not even cigarettes. I was too busy playing baseball and looking to make it to the Major Leagues. This false accusation created quite a dilemma, and I got into a big mess. The Police Department was questioning me about my relationship with this childhood friend, and it became a heavy load for me. I tried to call him more than 20 times, but he never picked up the phone. He had taken advantage of my friendship with him. I was deeply hurt, and it brought me to tears. I was broken. I would cry and cry before God daily. I was upset, angry, and sad at the same time. I had opened my heart to a so-called friend, and he had taken advantage of my position. Not only that, but this was also putting my family and me in a predicament. This situation didn't look good for me from any angle, and to clear my name, I had to hire a lawyer.

Lord, Remember Me?

While in this awful situation, I didn't know who to turn to. I remember being alone in my vehicle one day, going to court and calling on the name of the Lord for the first time in years. "Lord," I said, "remember me? If You still remember me, I need You." It had been three years since I had spoken to the Lord. I had been away from God and not even attending His house. I had been too busy with this world's cares and love for other things (Mark 4:19). That day, however, was my journey back home. I came back to my right mind while sitting alone inside my vehicle. Just like the prodigal son in Luke chapter 15 — who, after wasting his substance with riotous living, came suddenly into his right mind and realized that he had a better life awaiting him in his father's house — it was with me. I realized that the course of life that I had become interested in had pushed me to leave my Father's house. No, I was not womanizing, doing or selling drugs, smoking, drinking, or stealing. Still, I was lost. I was taking care of my family and had a good job. Yet, I was lost. I was a police officer and on the path to becoming a special agent with the FBI, but I was lost there. But the Lord is so gracious. In a moment, in that vehicle, I called out to the Lord and realized that He had never forgotten about me. Just like the father in scripture welcomed the son back home with joy and celebration, the Lord responded to me with open arms. I repented and came back home. The Presence of God flooded that vehicle as tears started flowing from my eyes. He worked immediately on my behalf and cleared my name from my accusers. This was in April 1995.

You see, I had backslidden and had forgotten about God. Though this was the second time I had wandered away since giving my life to the Lord Jesus back in college, I realized He never walked away from me. Neither did He abandon me. My friend, I want to encourage you that no matter what situation you find yourself in because of what you have done, God will never leave you. Our God is faithful. He will always be there for you, so take courage. Even though I did not call upon the name of God until I found myself in trouble, the same God who brought me supernaturally from my seat in the back of that little Baptist church in Texas heard me when I called and responded with His miracle-working power. The Lord had not forgotten me in all that time. And He will not forget you either!

> "This poor man cried out, and the Lord heard him, and saved him from all his troubles." (Psalms 34:6 NKJV)

Sometimes, God will allow certain circumstances into our lives to get our attention and bring us back to Himself again. His love is so real and fixed that it compels Him not to always bail us out of trouble. He often allows problems and uses them to draw us back to fellowship with Him.

"My son, despise not thou the chastening of the Lord, nor faint when thou art rebuked of him: For whom the Lord loveth he chasteneth, and scourgeth every son whom he receiveth" (Hebrews 12:5-6b KJV).

Today, I believe God allowed this challenging experience in my life to put me on the path of my destiny and for me to meet my Best Friend, the Holy Spirit.

Dear reader, please understand God knows how to get your attention. He has many ways to accomplish that. Also, know that His reason for getting your attention is always to bless you. His love endures forever. He will not remain angry forever. His mercies are new every day. Right now, I want to encourage you that no matter where you find yourself in life and how many or how deep your sins are, my Master, Jesus Christ, is ready and eager to forgive you. If you cry out to Him like I did that day, He will respond. His love for you is undeniable, unchangeable, and has no barriers to reaching you. He paid the ultimate price for your sins and mine. He gave up Himself for you. His love for you endures forever. Call upon Him right now. He will certainly hear you! Dear child of God, I am praying for you!

CHAPTER 9

When the Power Came
(How I Got Filled with the Holy Ghost)

Shortly after rededicating my life back to Christ, I became unemployed. I had a wife and a child to care for and rent to pay, but I had no money. My wife Carol was a social worker and the only one bringing in any income for our family of three. I was immensely bothered by this. Since I was a little boy, I always believed that a man should care for his family. Not being able to provide for mine was unacceptable to me. With this heaviness in my heart, I decided to call the prayer line of a popular Christian television program. "Hello, and God bless you! Thank you for calling the 700 Club. What is your prayer need?" The voice on the other side of the phone was about to change my life with a straightforward question. For those who don't know, the 700 Club still exists today and it still comes on the Christian network that created it. The man of God who started the network and hosted the show, Pat Robertson, has since gone home to be with Jesus, but the Lord has used him and the network he created to reach many and bring many to the foot of the Cross. God bless this man.

After the woman who picked up my call had asked me about my prayer request, she immediately followed with a question that changed my life. She said, *"Brother, have you received the Holy Spirit since you've believed?"* I had heard about the Holy Spirit but had not received Him. In my Christian walk, I did not know the difference between the "seal of the Spirit" and the "infilling of the Spirit." So, I responded to her and said, *"No."* Let me pause right here for a moment to explain. At that time, I believed in the Lord Jesus Christ. I was sealed with His Holy Spirit — meaning that the Holy Spirit had identified me as a believer and belonging to Christ Jesus. I WAS SEALED AS PART OF CHRIST'S INHERITANCE because I believed and had confessed that belief in Christ. I knew that from reading the Bible, but I did not immediately have the infilling of the Holy Spirit. This experience of being sealed and not immediately filled is common among people in the Church today. Yet, what is expected today was uncommon in the church of the Book of Acts. Let us understand that in the early church, the infilling of the Holy Spirit for a believer was synonymous with salvation. The apostolic church of the Book of Acts believed that all believers had to be filled with the Holy Spirit to walk in power and obey the Lord Jesus Christ. This infilling was their immediate experience, beginning in the upper room on the Day of Pentecost. Today, this is not practiced and believed among many in the Body of Christ. Therefore, many saved people cannot walk out their faith victoriously because they have not received the infilling of the Holy Spirit. How sad!

A Strange Sound Came Out Of My Mouth

Back to the phone call. The 700 Club phone line lady said, "*Okay, brother, let's pray.*" As she started to pray, I noticed that she began in English but then switched to what sounded like an Oriental language. I could not understand the language, but I knew it was Oriental. After praying in this unknown language, the woman prayed in English again. She asked God to fill me with the Holy Spirit. It was a short prayer. I thanked her, and we hung up.

Almost immediately after hanging up the phone, I began to have a strong urge to get down on my knees and worship God. Nobody was home but me that day, so I knelt in the middle of my living room floor and began to worship, praise, and thank God. I don't remember how long I did this, but I felt a sudden bubbly movement in my belly after some time. I had never experienced it before. I continued to worship Jesus Christ. Then, the strangest sound I had ever heard started to proceed out of my mouth without effort or even thinking of doing it. It started happening just like that! When I first heard it, it sounded like gibberish, which caused me to feel a little afraid, so I stopped. Then, inside me, I heard a voice that said, "Don't stop, continue." I started worshiping again, but every time I continued, this strange language would come out of my mouth whenever I opened it. Three times, the strange sound came from my mouth, and three times, I stopped. What was happening was different from any experience that I was familiar with. It seemed odd, but in my heart, I had an overwhelming peace and joy that was unspeakable and full of glory! I had read about this in the Bible but had not experienced it. The experience was all new to me.

After getting up from my knees, I realized that I had received the baptism of the Holy Spirit, with the evidence of speaking in other tongues! No one had laid hands on me. I received this baptism just like the 120 disciples on the Day of Pentecost. They had received it in the upper room, but I had received it in my living room!

> *"And they were all filled with the Holy Spirit and began to speak with other tongues, as the Spirit gave them utterance."* (Acts 2:4 NKJV)

I was so overjoyed. This strange language became stronger as I continued praying and praising God daily. It would flow easier out of my mouth. I was baptized with power from heaven. As days passed, I noticed that my prayer life got stronger, I could understand the Bible better, and my walking in obedience to what I read was better. I could feel power for living every single day. The infilling of the Holy Spirit changed my life forever. My encounter with heaven became more tangible, and Jesus became more real.

Speaking in tongues through the Holy Spirit is to speak again with the original language of how Adam talked to God. "What do you mean? Ed, are you saying that Adam spoke to God in gibberish?" No, of course not. That's not what I mean. To speak in tongues is to speak by the inspiration of the Spirit of God. Before Adam sinned against God, his method of communing with God was through the Holy Spirit, dwelling in him before he fell from grace because of disobedience. Paul said that he who speaks in tongues does not speak to man but unto God. (1 Corinthians 14:2)

This language is divine, holy, full of power, of the angelic realm, and full of mystery. It is the language of spiritual royalty, because we are a royal priesthood. Until the Tower of Babel, only one language was spoken on the earth, the language that derived from Adam. From this primary language came all other languages. That's why on the Day of Pentecost, the fire of the Spirit that settled upon each of them was "divided tongues" of fire, and that's why the multitude that were of different countries and spoke different languages could understand the speaking in tongues of the disciples when they came down to the street from the Upper Room (Acts 2:5-11). Follow me on what I'm about to tell you.

The language of the Spirit is the oldest language in the world and is the key that opens up God's mysteries (Acts 2:11). It unlocks the power to foretell/forthtell the future (prophesy) and see into the spirit world (visions and dreams) (Acts 2:17-18).

The language of the Spirit on the earth points to God's judgment that is to come (Acts 2:19-21). The Holy Spirit and tongues mean that God brought His Kingdom back to earth for the first time since Genesis 3 on the Day of Pentecost. It indicates that the fallen world is about to end, and God's renewal will come soon.

When a person filled with the Holy Spirit begins to speak in other tongues, some will ask what's going on, while others will be so far lost that they will mock this manifestation of God's Kingdom on earth (Acts 2:12-13). The Day of Pentecost was when

God's Spirit came down to seal our salvation, redemption, and future resurrection from death. He that is filled with the Spirit of Pentecost goes from eternal death to eternal life. Just like death could not keep Jesus because of God's Spirit in Him, the Spirit of God in us has loosed us from many things, such as sickness, disease, pain, and even death (Acts 2:22). I want to repeat this: the infilling of the Holy changed my life. It will change yours, too, if you receive Him and make Him your Best Friend. Hallelujah!

CHAPTER 10

"Pick It Up and Call"

After receiving the Holy Spirit's baptism, I started growing in many areas of my faith. I've been fortunate. I'm thankful to the Lord Jesus Christ for ordering my steps from when He called me to serve Him. Just like God used men in the Bible to train and mentor other men for the ministry, it was also with me. On a Saturday afternoon in April 1999, I was cleaning my office in the basement of my house. As I cleaned, I picked up a newspaper circular that had been put out of sight in one of my desk drawers a few weeks prior. Churches and ministries used this newspaper to advertise their upcoming services and events. As I took it, I noticed an advertisement that a church had placed about an upcoming event focused on deliverance and some deliverance classes offered at their theological institute. I read it and wasn't interested, so I threw it in the garbage pail and continued cleaning. Then I heard a gentle voice inside me say, "Pick it up and call."

I looked at the newspaper sitting inside the garbage pail and ignored it. Again, the same voice spoke from inside of me. This time, it sounded a bit louder but said the exact words, "Pick it up and call." Again, I looked at the garbage pail with the newspaper and ignored the instruction. I just wasn't interested. Then louder and with a much sterner sound, the very same voice said for the third time, "Pick it up and call!" As I heard this voice speaking with strict authority but also with love, I knew that this was the Holy Spirit speaking directly to me. I didn't understand why He wanted me to call and register, but later I would find out why.

When I called, a young lady picked up the phone. I told her I was calling about the deliverance classes that the ministry was offering. She immediately gave me information: location, dates, times, and the process to sign up for the classes. I thanked her for the information and hung up the phone. Thursday of that same week, I attended the deliverance class. Though I did not know it then, this moment was divine and connected with my introduction and exposure to the deliverance ministry that the Lord had given me through spiritual dreams for many years. Again, without knowing it, I had entered the next phase of spiritual training that God was using to prepare me for what was to come in my calling. It would put me on the path to my destiny and bring me to know the man who would ultimately take me under his wing, become my spiritual father in the ministry, introduce me to the Holy Spirit as a Person, and teach me so many things that I would need to know in my ministry later.

During those days, I had no idea that God has a perfect plan and purpose for all of us or that His plans and calling regarding us have been perfectly blueprinted and predestinated since before the foundation of the world. I had no understanding that our calling is ordained before we are even formed in our mothers' wombs.

> *"Then the word of the Lord came to me, saying: 'Before I formed you in the womb, I knew you; Before you were born I sanctified you; I ordained you a prophet to the nations.'"*
> (Jeremiah 1:4-5 NKJV)

Making that phone call that Saturday afternoon changed the whole course of my life. The Holy Spirit knows you by name. He has a perfect and unfailing plan for your purpose and future. He is the only one who can reveal it, guide you to it, and help you fulfill it. Without Him, we are helpless — lost, not knowing why we are here or what we were born to do. But, with the Holy Spirit at the steering wheel of your life, guiding your steps and directing your actions, you will know the answers to life's questions of destiny and purpose. Once you walk with Him in total surrender and intimacy, get ready to ride the most incredible train of revelation and discovery about your reason for being born that anybody has ever known. He is the key to getting to your destination in life.

So, ready for the ride?

CHAPTER 11

Dreams, Dreams, and More Dreams

My initial ministerial training did not occur in a theological seminary or Bible college, though I have theological training. However, I was first taught in the College of the Holy Spirit. As I mentioned, when the Lord called me, He immediately introduced me to the supernatural realm via dreams. The Holy Spirit is the dream-giver of heaven, and these dreams were preparation for what was to come. In the Bible, God showed many of His great servants their future ministries through visions and dreams. Joseph is an excellent example of this:

> *"And Joseph dreamed a dream, and he told it to his brethren: and they hated him yet the more. And he said unto them, Hear, I pray you, this dream which I have dreamed: For, behold, we were binding sheaves in the field, and, lo, my sheaf arose, and also stood upright; and behold, your sheaves stood round about, and made obeisance to my sheaf. And his brethren said to him, Shalt thou indeed reign over us? Or shalt thou indeed have dominion over us? And they hated*

him yet the more for his dreams and for his words." (Genesis 37:5-8 KJV)

As it was then, so it is now. Even today, the Holy Spirit reveals future ministries and callings through dreams. Over eighteen years, beginning directly after my conversion, I had more than fifty dreams concerning what God was calling me to do in the future. Though I did not understand many of the dreams when I first dreamt them, today I see that all those dreams were preparing my spirit for what was to come. Throughout those years, I saw myself in dreams preaching in stadiums, healing the sick, casting out demons, and fighting spiritual battles against the forces of darkness. Let me share one of them with you.

In one of the dreams I had, I saw myself in a classroom. The teacher was a famous evangelist by the name of Reinhard Bonnke who had won over 80 million people for Christ through his ministry. As I sat in the classroom, Evangelist Bonnke was the teacher. I sat behind my desk, listening to the lesson that he was teaching. When the class finished, I went out of the classroom, and I saw the setting was in a village in Africa. Evangelist Bonnke also came outside. He looked at me. He laid his hand on my head and walked away, leaving the village. Later in my life, I was called out to the evangelistic ministry, and thousands of people started to attend my international crusades, and hundreds gave their lives to Christ.

Much of what God has called me to do and I have done, I began to see it in my dreams. Had it not been for the ministry of the Holy Spirit speaking to me in dreams, I don't know where I would be with my life and ministry today. The Bible tells us that when the Holy Spirit comes upon a person, one of the things that will happen is they will dream dreams (Acts 2:17).

CHAPTER 12

Satan Made the Bride Cry

One day, I had a dream that I was walking inside what appeared to be an underground car garage. Suddenly, I was confronted by three individuals whose appearances were like men, but their characteristics were evil and devious. In the dream, I knew that these three men were evil spirits. One of them started to attack me. I fought back — rebuking him in the name of Jesus. Within one minute, I defeated him and saw the ground swallow him. Likewise, the second one attacked me. This one had just a bit more power than the first one, so it took me a little longer to defeat him. But, just like the first, after rebuking him in the name of Jesus with power and faith, he was beaten and swallowed by the ground. When he saw that I had defeated the other two, the third one, who appeared to be their leader, came against me.

We started fighting, and I noticed his strength was more significant than the others. The fights in this dream weren't with hands or physical weapons but with spiritual weapons and through the spoken word. This third attacker was resisting at all costs the rebuke I was commanding in the name of Jesus.

Then, from the depth of my being, with anger in my spirit, I raised my voice with faith and determination, saying, "In the name of Jesus Christ of Nazareth, I bind you!" Suddenly, it was as if a force had taken him. The ground opened and swallowed him, just like what happened with the other two. I then left the underground garage. Next, I found myself walking down a particular street. After going about two blocks, I saw a coffin being carried out of a place to my left. I approached those who were taking it and asked to look inside. They stopped and opened the lid of the coffin. When I looked inside, I saw the dead body of a man. I disliked what I saw and rejected it as I said "No" and continued. I walked to the end of the street and saw a two-story white house. I stopped and looked towards it. A young, beautiful lady in a white wedding dress was leaning out the second-story window and crying. I shouted to her, asking why she was crying. She didn't answer me. I asked her again, "Why are you crying on your most special day? You are about to get married! You shouldn't be crying; you should be happy." But she just kept on crying. As I stood there, I thought her crying was because of who was standing behind her inside the room. I sensed this entity was causing her to cry when she should have been happy to be about to get married. She was leaning out the window and the only one I could see in the room. I wanted to see the face of the one responsible for her tears. "You, standing behind her inside the room, and who is responsible for making this woman cry, reveal yourself," I commanded. I said this twice. Then, a creature emerged from the same window and showed its face. It was in the form of a man but had animal features. The creature resembled a dragon and was wearing a crown on his head. I asked him, "Who is making this woman cry?"

"I am," he replied defiantly. He sounded arrogant and as if he was enjoying it. "I am a king and don't want her to be happy!"

"Okay," I said. "In the name of Jesus Christ, my Lord, I command you to cast yourself down from the window and fall to the ground." I gave this command three times. Then, it was as if a giant, invisible hand came behind him and pushed him out the second-floor window. The creature fell to the ground at my feet, and I was suddenly awakened from the dream. My then four-year-old son called my name because he had just woken up and was hungry.

Many years later, after growing up in the Lord and being ordained into the ministry, I understood the dream's meaning. It spoke of the Bride of Christ, who will soon be married to her Bridegroom, Jesus Christ, and how Satan is harassing her to the shedding of tears. I understood that my God had called me to free the Church from her oppressor and prepare her before her Bridegroom's return. If you are a minister of Christ — whether an apostle, prophet, evangelist, pastor, or teacher — please, I encourage you to understand that the sole purpose for which the Lord Jesus Christ has called you and ordained you into the five-fold ministry is to prepare His Bride (the Church) before the Marriage Supper of the Lamb (Revelation 19:9). Jesus is indeed coming back. He will receive His Bride unto Himself, so that where He is, she may also be. (John. 14:2)

As I continued growing in the things of the ministry, I also realized that the realm of the spirit is very complex to navigate in my strength. I realized that I needed help to do it properly.

Thankfully, God is faithful. He always allows things to happen in your life so that you move to the next level of what He's calling you to do. He always has a plan and knows how to order your steps to get you there — even if He must allow the devil to show up and harass you.

> *"The steps of a good man are ordered by the Lord, and He delights in his way. Though he falls, he shall not be utterly cast down; for the Lord upholds him with His hand."* (Psalms 37:23-24 NKJV)

CHAPTER 13

Lucifer Walks into My Room

One day, the church I was serving had a mass deliverance service at one of our satellite branches in Schenectady, New York. People came from different cities and churches to receive deliverance from evil spirits tormenting them. During the event, as my spiritual father began praying out loud, rebuking the spirits by name, one sister who had come for deliverance began to manifest an evil spirit by screaming and rolling on the ground. I went to help her be delivered. A battle started as I laid my hands on her and commanded the evil spirit to leave. Here's how it went:

Demon: [Screaming angrily and sneering at me] "Citronnelli, get your hand off me!"

Me: "Come out of her and let her go!"

Demon: "No, I'm not coming out. Now, get your hand off of me."

Me: "Shut up and come out, in Jesus' name!"

Demon: "No, you shut up! I'm not leaving. You're not strong enough. Get out of here. You're weak."

By this time, many people who had looked up to me as being able to cast out demons were looking at what was ensuing. Instead of concentrating my faith in Jesus, I became self-conscious. I wondered, "What will these people think of me if I can't cast out this evil spirit from this sister?" What a big mistake. But, at the time, I didn't know that, as I needed to be more mature in the deliverance ministry. Instead of disengaging and calling my spiritual father, who was more mature in this type of deliverance than I was and had a higher anointing, I continued to engage. What came next almost killed my ministry before it even started.

Demon: "I entered her through the fragrance of a cologne from our kingdom. We gave the recipe to one of our agents, who is homosexual. He made it, and now it is on the market. Thousands of men have purchased it and are using it. When they use it, we enter the woman who smells it if they're weak-minded because the spirit of lust is planted in it. When it happens, she begins to lust after the man in her mind when she smells it."

By this time, not only were the people curious and listening, but so was I. The demon was revealing secrets of the underworld.

Sometimes, the Holy Spirit forces demons to reveal their tactics to us against their will so that we may be more effective against their kingdom. Let me add something right here about this. Sometimes, while in a deliverance session with a person, I am led by the Spirit to question the demon. The demon will then begin to speak through the person. At times, some people ask why I do this. They say that Jesus never told us to talk to demons because demons are all liars. "Just cast them out!" they exclaim.

Please understand that though it is the devil's nature to lie constantly, there are times in deliverance ministry when the Holy Spirit will force the evil spirit to reveal something true. They do not do this because they want to tell the truth but because God causes them to speak. He pushes this to happen so we may hear things about them that we would never know otherwise. These things can help affect the deliverance of the person. Again, the nature of evil spirits is to lie. Still, there are times when they are forced to reveal a secret, such as their name or information about their operation. Even Jesus questioned demons in the Bible — not because He needed to, but so that it could be written in scripture and so that we, who are His followers, could learn from it.

> *"Then He asked him, what is your name? and he answered, saying, my name is Legion, for we are many."* (Mark 5:9 NKJV)

Now, let me go back to the story. Knowing that people looked up to me in the ministry of deliverance and being unable to cast out this demon made me self-conscious. I felt discouraged and embarrassed. My faith went from me, and I wanted to save face. When this happened, the Holy Spirit was no longer doing the work through me. It was now me working in the flesh. I was not able to drive this one out.

Let me pause again and encourage you who are reading this book. Please realize that you are fighting an unseen war with an unseen enemy. This enemy does not operate by human standards or natural strength. Understand that his ability comes from another dimension that puts you and me at a disadvantage as genuine human beings. Please know you are no match for this unseen enemy in your natural strength. You and I need the power of God's Spirit to overcome this enemy. Look at what the scriptures say about this:

> *"So he answered and said to me: "This is the word of the Lord to Zerubbabel: 'Not by might nor by power, but by My Spirit,' says the Lord of hosts." (Zechariah 4:6 NKJV)*

> *"But if I cast out demons by the Spirit of God, surely the kingdom of God has come upon you." (Matthew 12:28 NKJV)*

> *"I am the vine, you are the branches. He who abides in Me, and I in him, bears much fruit; for without Me you can do nothing." (John 15:5 NKJV)*

Did you get that? Defeating the enemy is impossible without the Holy Spirit's power. I was devastated. I felt I had failed God and His people, whom He had sent me to deliver. I felt as if I did not belong in ministry at all. I felt God had made a mistake calling me into the ministry, and I wanted to go away and hide somewhere. I began to think about how the disciples felt in Matthew chapter 17. Jesus had given them the authority to cast out devils. Still, after seeing success in exercising this authority, they found themselves unable to cast the demon out of a young boy. Look at this exchange between them and the Master after this failure:

> *"Then, the disciples came to Jesus privately and said, 'Why could we not cast it out?' So, Jesus said to them, 'Because of your unbelief; for assuredly, I say to you, if you have faith as a mustard seed, you will say to this mountain, "Move from here to there," and it will move, and nothing will be impossible for you. However, this kind does not go out except by prayer and fasting.'" (Matthew 17:19-21 NKJV)*

CHAPTER 14

The Day Everything Changed

It was 6:00 p.m. on a Saturday in October 2005, and everything was about to change. After the service, my spiritual parents, Bishop and Mother Bryant Sr., returned to their hotel room to rest. I went back to mine to sulk. I was so discouraged that I didn't want to eat. As soon as I entered the hotel room, I fell on the bed and cried out to God. After a few minutes of crying on the bed, I felt a dreadful, cold presence entering the room. I did not know what it was, but I knew it was not good. As this entity entered the room, fear and darkness followed behind him. Not coming near me, it walked over to one of the corners of the room and stood there looking at me. I did not see this entity with my literal physical eyes. Still, spiritually, I knew for sure that it was standing there. This presence's oppression almost choked my breath, and my heart began to race. Fear tried to overtake me, and it was winning. This force was not of this world. The air became cold with a cold I could feel in my bones, and an unimaginable hatred for God and me flooded the room. I didn't know what to do. I wanted to run to my spiritual father across the hallway but could not move. I was paralyzed with fear. I started calling on the Name of the Lord and crying to God, but I heard no response from Him. The dark figure in the corner of the room continued staring at me. After a few minutes, I knew that this was Satan himself.

I began to hear him laugh. His voice wasn't audible. It was spiritual. I listened to the laughter in my mind, even though he was standing in the corner of the room. He began to project words into my mind that were not my thoughts. Without opening his mouth, he would channel his thoughts into my mind.

> *Satan:* "Tell that Man up there that He made a mistake with you. Tell Him that you are not cut out for this."

As I heard him speak to my mind from the corner of the room, all I knew to do was cry to God for help.

> *Me:* "God, where are You?"

No answer came. God was silent.

> *Satan:* "Tell Him to release you from ministry. Tell Him that you can't do this."

> *Me:* "God, where are You? Please help me."

I continued to cry out to God. Tears were running down my cheeks. But again, no answer.

Satan: "Tell Him that others He chose could do it, but not you."

Me: "God, where are You? Please help me. I need You. I can't do this without You. Please help me."

Throughout the night, I found myself as if I was walking through the shadow of death and feeling the piercing of darkness. There were moments when I would fall asleep crying and calling out to God, but Satan would wake me up with mocking and accusations within ten minutes. It was grueling. I felt worn out. All I could say was, "God, help me." I didn't know it then, but today, I understand that Satan was trying to get me to willingly forfeit my assignment on the earth by calling God a liar. He was trying to get me to abort my ministry by telling God that I was unfit for ministry and that He had made a mistake by calling me.

The spiritual battle was intense. It was unlike anything that I had ever encountered. Satan stood in the room for nearly twelve hours, tempting me to sin against God with my mouth. Later, I began to understand the predicament of Job in the Bible. Satan was probably pressuring Job to sin against God with his mouth, but the Bible says Job never did.

"*In all this did not Job sin with his lips.*" (Job 2:10 KJV)

"You Have Passed The Test"

I woke up at 6:30 a.m. after remaining asleep for about one hour. Only this time, I wasn't awakened by Satan. Jesus, the

Master Himself, the King of Kings, Lord of Lords, my Savior and deliverer, had walked into the room with a pure white robe! The cold and the fear were gone. The room felt lighter, and there was a sense of peace. There was no more darkness and heaviness. Darkness must flee when light shows up! Satan had left when Jesus, the Light of the World, had walked in. "You have passed the test," the Lord Jesus told me.

"Lord, test? What test?" I questioned.

"Though you were being tormented by Satan and being forced to sin with your mouth against Me, not once did you deny Me. Not once did you say that I made a mistake and to release you from the ministry. That's why you passed the test." With that, my Master, Jesus, walked out of the room. The storm had passed. The piercing darkness had fled and given way to peace and light. Hallelujah!

Whether you are an ordained minister of Jesus Christ or a layperson in the church, there will be times when, no matter how hard you try, it will seem as if you have failed at what God has called you to do. I want you to know that no, you have not failed. God may be allowing some things in your life to happen so that you can learn more profound things and get stronger so that He may use you more powerfully later to help more people. Know that Jesus does not make any mistakes when He chooses someone for His glory. The devil is the accuser of the brethren. He's the one who makes you feel defeated when you make a small mistake. Satan is the one who brings condemnation, not God. The Lord Jesus will never condemn you, even when you make a mistake. He loves you and cares for you. He wants you to succeed at everything you do. Whatever we do for God, we do by grace. Never forget that God knew before He called you that there would be times when you would fall flat on your face. Yet, knowing this did not prevent Him from choosing you. He that calls you is faithful and will not allow you to be put to shame. He takes our failures and turns them into a success story. He takes our tests and turns them into a testimony. He takes our disappointments and makes them divine appointments that bless many. He allows you to go through the valley of the shadow of death so that He can show His delivering power. There is no failure in God. I learned this after that experience with that demon of doubt. Today, because of my dependency on the Holy Spirit, I see the glory and power of God in a more unprecedented way. Today, I know that He will be there to catch me if I fail. Child of God, if He does it for me, He will also do it for you—glory to His name.

CHAPTER 15

"Follow Him"

"'Call to Me, and I will answer you, and show you great and mighty things, which you do not know.'"
(Jeremiah 33:3 NKJV)

Following this unforgettable experience, I began to understand the depth to which my life as a minister of Christ was powerless without the Holy Spirit, powerless to the point that it was finished even before it could truly begin. The man who became my father in the faith has since gone home to be with the Lord. The Lord called Bishop Roy Bryant, Sr., as a young man. He started his ministry evangelizing the hospitals of New York City, where God used him in miracles and healing. As he went out and ministered to those sick — even sick unto death — many got healed by the power of Jesus Christ. His church started to grow as the people who had received healing and salvation after being prayed for by him began to attend his services and became a part of his congregation. They called it "the church that came out of the hospital." The ministries of healing and deliverance always go together, and the Lord also began to manifest deliverance through his ministry. God sent me this man to be my spiritual father. He used him to teach, train, and mentor me, giving me a foundation I would later need for my ministry. There was a time after being ordained into the ministry when I found myself making many ministerial mistakes, both in the general church and in deliverance. I am intelligent, with an average I.Q. and a Bachelor of Science in Organizational Management. Even so, the mistakes I was making were causing significant problems. Often, my spiritual father would call me to point out my errors — not in a rebuking way — to teach me and to let me know that I was not doing things correctly. Sometimes, he informed me that he'd had to defend me against other church leaders because of these mistakes. I felt terrible. I became desperate to change but couldn't figure out how. I was feeling discouraged before God showed up with a solution.

"Follow Him" Dream

Because of all the mistakes that I was making, I sought the Lord in prayer and fasting so that He would show me the way out of the cycle and how to correct my errors. A few days later, I had a dream. I was flying close to the clouds and over a clear body of water. It was a clear day. I saw three other individuals flying together with me. They looked like men with white robes. I was flying in front of them, and they were next to me, on my left and on my right. I saw a pure white dove flying towards me from my right side. It got in front of me for a little while, and suddenly, the dove descended into the water beneath and was traveling under the water in the same direction we were. From my altitude, I could see it moving underwater. Then I heard a voice from the cloud saying, "Follow Him!" I descended into the water to follow the dove. We were now under the crystal clear water. We came up to a wall that had an opening with iron bars. I saw the white dove go through and into the other side. I tried to go through, but I could not because I was too physically big. There was no way. The dove came over to the opening and, looking at me through the iron bars, spoke to me. I could hear His Words in my mind. It said, "Look to your left-hand side." I looked and saw a bigger opening that I could fit through. I went there and got to the other side, and then I woke up from the dream.

This dream not only gave me the answer to why I was making all those mistakes but also showed me the key to a life of victory, success, fruitfulness, increase, happiness, joy, and dominion! In other words, this dream showed me that the Holy Spirit of God is the key to living God's plan and intent for us since the beginning of creation.

> *"Then God blessed them and God said to them, 'Be fruitful and multiply; fill the earth and subdue it; have dominion over the fish of the sea, over the birds of the air, and every living thing that moves on the earth.'"* (Genesis 1:28 NKJV)

Yes, my friend, God's plan and will are and always have been for man to be fruitful and multiply in all his endeavors. It is God's will and plan for man to subdue and have dominion over his environment and to live a life of abundance, success, and power. How was man supposed to accomplish what God had said of him? How was man to have dominion over all things and to live a life of greatness on the earth? The answer is in Genesis 2:7 NKJV. Let's look at the Word of God again:

> *"And the Lord God formed man of the dust of the ground and breathed into his nostrils the breath of life; and man became a living being."*

God breathed Himself inside of man. The verse calls it *"the breath of life."* The meaning of the word breath in the context of the original Hebrew language is "Spirit." In other words, God breathed His Spirit inside man when He created him. Since God is Spirit, God breathed Himself inside of man. So, by nature, man carries God's DNA of life and power — the Holy Spirit. Sin deactivated, neutralized, and paralyzed this divine essence within man. Only when man returns to his Maker through a relationship with Jesus Christ can God's DNA be reactivated by the same Holy Spirit who gave man breath in Genesis. To return to this position of dominion and power is to go back to the abundant life described in John 10:10. Returning to that condition requires repentance of sin, believing in the Lord Jesus Christ for the forgiveness of sin through His blood, and the infilling of the Holy Spirit of Life. The Holy Spirit is the secret to the life of an overcomer. You and I need that *"breath"* of God again in our bodies for us to reign, succeed, and be victorious in life. We need His power and wisdom to triumph over failure, defeat, sickness, poverty, and limitations. The Holy Spirit is the key to reigning in life as God's original plan intended. I praise the Lord and thank God for the Holy Spirit!

CHAPTER 16

The Secret Place of Power

It was in my prayer room, in the tiny basement of my house, that I got to know my Best Friend. As I spent time alone with the Holy Spirit, we laughed, we cried together, He spoke of things to come, and He taught me some things about myself that I did not know. Many things He showed me in those special times alone would later shape my ministry.

To be with the Holy Spirit is to have access to the mysteries of the universe. He will teach you things that you could have never imagined. When He speaks, one word from His mouth will result in a life-changing experience. To find Him is to get to know Him; to know Him is to find life itself.

There is a deep, intimate place in God open to all who choose it. Yet, only a few people find it. This place is secret. This place is hidden. However, this place is accessible. Two thousand years ago, a way was made for us to enter through the Body of Jesus Christ by the power of the Holy Spirit. The Bible says the following about what happened when Jesus died on the Cross:

"Jesus, when he had cried again with a loud voice, yielded up the ghost. And, behold, the veil of the temple was rent in

twain from the top to the bottom." (Matthew 27:50-51a KJV)

This tearing of the veil is very significant for every believer. This tearing gave every believer access to the Secret Place of God once and for all. The Bible speaks of a tabernacle God told Moses to build in Exodus. The Lord gave Moses precise instructions on constructing this dwelling meant to house His Glory while the children of Israel were in the wilderness. The tabernacle consisted of four areas: the gate, the outer court, the inner court, and the Most Holy Place. It was in this area called the Most Holy Place that the Ark of the Covenant was kept, and it was here that the Presence of God dwelt. Because it was such a revered place, God had commanded that no one could enter there except the high priest, once a year. The high priest could not come into the Presence of God whenever or however he wanted. He needed to follow a specific pattern of instructions to fulfill God's ordained requirement for the tabernacle.

This tabernacle in the wilderness was only a shadow pointing to Christ and what He would accomplish for us through the finished work of the Cross. Even so, the tabernacle and the path and protocols for operating it are clear descriptions that point us to intimacy with the Holy Spirit.

The Entrance Gate: Jesus Is The Door

> "For the Gate of the court, there shall be a screen twenty cubits long, woven of blue, purple, and scarlet thread, and fine woven linen, made by a weaver. It shall have four pillars and four sockets." (Exodus 27:16 NKJV)

Everyone who wanted to pursue the Presence of God in the time of the tabernacle, whether a sinner seeking forgiveness or a priest making atonement, had to enter through the same gate: The gate of entrance. This gate, being the narrowest, was the only way to enter the tabernacle, and it led to the Holy of Holies (the place of the Presence of the Lord). Once a man entered this gate, he was on holy ground. The gate was on the east side of the camp of the children of Israel and was strategically located where the Tribe of Judah was camped. Judah was the kingly tribe, and its name meant "praise."

This entrance door represents Christ. He is the door to salvation (John 10:9). "Jesus said, 'I am the way; the truth, and the life, and no man comes to the Father, except by me.'" (John 14:6 NKJV) Through repentance and praise, we come through the door of Jesus and into salvation.

The Outer Court: Jesus Is The Perfect Sacrifice

Once a person entered the tabernacle, they would find themselves in the outer court. Here, they would see two bronze furnishings — the laver and the bronze altar — representing judgment and sin. The bronze altar was the first stop a priest would make. This altar was made of acacia wood and covered in bronze, with a horn on each corner. The animal to be sacrificed would be tied down to these horns while awaiting the moment of its perishing. Innocent blood needed to be shed before a priest could enter the Most Holy Place. This blood was the price for the judgment of sin. This animal with no spot, blemish, or other imperfection which had to shed its blood for the priest to move forward represents Jesus himself. Christ's shed blood is what qualifies us for what is next.

After the bronze altar, the priest would come to the laver. The laver was made entirely of bronze. It had a base and an open top where water was kept. After the sacrifice at the bronze altar, the priest had to go to the laver and wash his hands and feet before entering the inner court of the tabernacle. A priest could only move forward and minister by completing this step. If he failed to, the result would be death in the holy Presence of the Lord. Thankfully for us today, this was fulfilled in Jesus as well. Christ's death and resurrection gave us the washing of the water of the Word (Ephesians 5:26). His Word and the power of the Holy Spirit have cleansed and regenerated us.

The Holy Place: Jesus, The Bread From Heaven

The priest then went through the first curtain into the inner court or the Holy Place, occupied by the golden lampstand, the incense altar, and the table of showbread. The golden lampstand (menorah) was beaten and fashioned out of a single block of gold and had three branches coming out of each side of a central shaft. The seven lamps on top of the branches were likely round saucers with pinched rims that held wicks and olive oil. Every morning and every evening in the Holy Place, the priest would offer a mixture of frankincense and other aromatic resins while tending the menorah's light. The table of showbread was made of acacia wood and overlaid with pure gold. A gold ring near each corner of the table was near its leg where the two acacia poles, also plated in gold, would be inserted to carry the table.

The plates, dishes, pitchers, and bowls used on this table were all pure gold. There were always to be twelve loaves of bread on this table before the Lord, which were to be changed by the priest every Sabbath. This bread was "from the people of Israel as a covenant forever." (Leviticus 24:8 ESV) In this, we see Jesus, who established God's new and better covenant by shedding His blood and resurrection from the dead.

The Holy Of Holies – The Secret Place

Beyond the inner court was the Holy of Holies. The priest could enter here only once yearly, on the Day of Atonement. It was where the Ark of the Covenant was housed. The Ark was covered by the "mercy seat," upon which the high priest sprinkled the blood of the sacrificial goat seven times. The Ark represented the footstool of God's throne. When Jesus cried with a loud voice and yielded His Spirit to die, this cry released a mighty wave in Jerusalem that went from the hill of Golgotha, where Christ was crucified, all the way to the temple, where the curtain covering the entrance to the Holy of Holies was suddenly split in two from top to bottom, opening this secret place. (Matthew 27:50-51) Jesus' death on the Cross opened the way to the Presence of the Lord for every believer who chooses to pursue it. So why is it a secret? Because the Presence of the Lord is a vast, profound mystery. Only the Spirit of the Lord truly knows the way to navigate it. It took God to open the way for us to come into the Presence of God. In the same way, it takes the Spirit of God to navigate us into the Presence and Glory of God. Thus, scripture tells us that the Holy Spirit searches the deep things of God and makes them known to us:

> "But God hath revealed them unto us by his Spirit: for the Spirit searcheth all things, yea, the deep things of God." (1 Corinthians 2:10 KJV)

As a pastor with a growing church and a thriving international ministry, my schedule can become quite full, and I can find myself being extended some exciting opportunities. Still, I'd rather be alone in my little prayer room. Doing the work of the Lord and seeing Him display His mighty power is exciting. Still, I'd rather be communing with the Holy Spirit than be preaching in a crusade or a service. To be with Him is to experience an ecstasy born in heaven. To feel His Presence and smell His fragrance is to be caught up in a place outside of time. Oh, how I long for His company and His fellowship. To me, to think about a life without Him is not to have a purpose for living. He is the greatest Friend in the world, and this Friend reveals Himself in the Secret Place.

Your Secret Is Safe With Him

To know the Holy Spirit is to understand the Father and the Son. It is to know a Person who is all-powerful yet the most sensitive. To know Him is to know the One that manifested what the spoken Word said in the beginning. The Presence of the Holy Spirit emanates the love of Christ, which surpasses all human comprehension. The more you get to know Him, the more you fall in love with Him. He is a trusted Friend and a Brother. In Him is a sense of safety and security. You can share with Him any secret, though He knows the innermost secrets of your heart even before you tell Him. As you spend time with Him, you can rest assured that your secrets are safe with Him. Your deepest thoughts, needs, weaknesses, and longings are all safe with Him. The Holy Spirit will never betray you. He moves in the intentions and plans of God towards you always.

Beloved, the Holy Spirit is a trusted companion, counselor, and confidant. He is all-wise. As you follow His wisdom and instructions, you will always go right. To know Him is to know love, peace, laughter, security, joy, and protection. To know Him is to know the most significant, extraordinary, greatest Person in the world.

CHAPTER 17

First the Spirit, Then the Voice

I made many mistakes when I started because I did not know Him. As I walk with Him many years later, I still learn about Him. Every day is a learning experience for me with Him. I'm forever in the classroom of the Holy Spirit. One day, while I studied the scriptures, I was reading the passage in Matthew 3:16-17 NKJV:

> *When He had been baptized, Jesus came up immediately from the water; and behold, the heavens were opened to Him, and He saw the Spirit of God descending like a dove and alighting upon Him. And suddenly a voice came from heaven, saying, "This is My beloved Son, in whom I am well pleased."*

I read that, and His voice within me said, "Turn now and read Genesis 1:1-3." I turned there and read:

> *In the beginning God created the heavens and the earth. The earth was without form, and void; and darkness was on the*

face of the deep. And the Spirit of God was hovering over the face of the waters. Then God said, "Let there be light"; and there was light. (NKJV)

Suddenly, I saw in those two passages something I had never seen before. I saw that God never spoke before His Spirit was present. It was after the Holy Spirit showed up that God followed with His Word, saying what He said. I realized that God depended on His Spirit to empower His Word. I realized that day the Holy Spirit creates the atmosphere for the Word. It is His Presence that energizes the Word and makes it alive. Immediately, I saw three things about the Spirit and the Word. One, anything God is about to do, including during creation, involves three Persons: the Father, the Word, and the Spirit.

"For there are three that bear witness in heaven: the Father, the Word, and the Holy Spirit; and these three are one." (1 John 5:7 NKJV)

We see all three here "bearing witness" or bearing record" together in heaven. The word "witness" is the word *"martyreo,"* which means someone who has evidence or knowledge and can give a report of something they have seen or heard. You noticed that the above word is a compound word, "marty-reo." The root Greek word is "martys," which is where we get the word "martyr." A martyr is *a person who voluntarily suffers death as the penalty of witnessing and refuses to renounce what he has believed or seen.*

The Bible tells us that Jesus (the Word/the Lamb of God) was slain before the foundation of the world.

"And all that dwell upon the earth shall worship him, whose names are not written in the book of life of the Lamb slain from the foundation of the world." (Revelation 13:8 KJV)

My friend, Jesus, as the Word in eternity past, witnessed the suffering of humanity before it even happened. Before man disobeyed his maker, all three of the Godhead saw what would happen before it happened. So, all three bore witness in heaven of this. And the Word volunteered to take on flesh (John 1:14) and die for humanity to save them before humanity was even humanity. When the Word witnessed this terrible situation, to redeem His creation, the Word proceeded out of the bosom of the Father, and the Holy Spirit moved upon the Word, giving him a human body. The Word became human like those He had created. God never speaks or acts independently of His Spirit. In Genesis chapter 1, during creation, we see that the Holy Spirit moved first, then God said, "Let there be light." In Matthew chapter 3, we see Jesus (the Word) coming out of the water, the heavens opening, the Holy Spirit descending (moving), and then God saying, *"This is My beloved Son, in whom I am well pleased."*

This Is The Secret: His Atmosphere

So, you see, it was always when the Holy Spirit arrived that God spoke, not before. I want you to know this and always remember it. The Holy Spirit is the one that creates the atmosphere that incubates, energizes, and empowers what you say. It is all about the atmosphere. You must have a connection and a close association with Him for His atmosphere and His Presence to move upon your words to carry the power to create changes in your life and around those God is sending you to. If God has called you to ministry, I want you to know that the Holy Spirit has been given to you to bring life and changes to your world and others around you. As God never speaks outside of His atmosphere, which His Spirit brings, I encourage you to be mindful of that. Follow the same pattern; you will see mighty things when you speak for God. The Holy Spirit is the key that empowers God's Word in your life and ministry. These two, fused together, will change your life.

CHAPTER 18

The Secret to Your Success

Many years ago, there was a movie titled *The Secret of my Success*, with Michael J. Fox. I loved that movie, and I watched it multiple times, because the moral of the story was that a poor kid from Kansas wound up becoming the CEO of a major company. There's more to the story, but you must watch it to find out. Everyone who comes to Jesus Christ confessing their sins receives His love and forgiveness for their sins; salvation is granted immediately. From that time on, the Holy Spirit gives you the ability, strength, and will to obey God and live the Christian life if you submit to Him. No one can obey God and submit to His commandments without the help of the Holy Spirit. It is humanly impossible. We need a change of heart first, and He's the only one with the power to do that in us.

> *"I will give you a new heart and put a new spirit within you; I will take the heart of stone out of your flesh and give you a heart of flesh. I will put My Spirit within you and cause you to walk in My statutes, and you will keep My judgments and do them."* (Ezekiel 36:26-27 NKJV)

Many people struggle to walk with Christ and live an abundant life because they fail to understand that their flesh is weak and cannot depend on their human abilities. They say, "I can smoke and do drugs, drink alcohol, watch pornography, but I'll never be addicted; that happens to the other person, but not me," until they find themselves caught up in the same destructive addictions. Understand that without His help, you are helpless against the flesh. Without Him, you cannot even pray, read the Word, pay tithes, or anything. Only with the help of the Holy Spirit can you and I make it in this life. He is the one who has been given to you to help you succeed in every area of your life. When you walk with the Holy Spirit, He not only enables you to overcome temptation, but He shows you how to succeed in business, marriage, and financial management. He shows you how to get out of debt, how to lead your children and succeed in ministry. If you have been called to ministry, He will give you strategies for how to grow your ministry and church, and He will draw the people to you. Power will be released in your services, and people will visit your church looking for healing, deliverance, miracles, and a Word from God. Oh, my friend, He is the answer you've been looking for. You don't have to struggle anymore. God has sent the Spirit of His Son to make you a sign and a wonder on the earth for His glory. He sent His Spirit so that you can be an example of what God meant man should be from the beginning of time. The Holy Spirit has become to me the greatest person and Best Friend in the world. If you spend time with Him, you will get to know Him. He wants to be known of you. If you call on Him, He will come. If you ask Him a question, He will answer you.

One day, I found myself a bit discouraged because the ministry was not growing the way it should have. We were struggling financially, and people were not coming to the services. If they did come once or twice, they didn't come back, so as a result, the church was not growing. I began to seek the Holy Spirit for an answer. In prayer, I asked Him, "Lord, why isn't the church growing? Why are people not coming and staying? What am I doing wrong?" The whole night, I prayed, asking the same question. In those days, I didn't know that He spoke in different ways.

"God, who at various times and in various ways spoke in time past to the fathers by the prophets," (Hebrews 1:1 NKJV)

The Anointing Needs The Right Infrastructure

Suddenly, I heard inside my heart, in my spirit, His voice saying to me, "The anointing alone does not grow the church."

I said, "What? The anointing alone does not grow the church?" I thought I was hearing things. I always thought that the anointing was all you needed for people to come, stay, and grow the church.

He repeated it to me, "The anointing alone does not grow the church; it is a combination of the anointing working with the correct infrastructure that grows the church."

I understood that He is the one who grows the church by showing the person what to do. I heard, "The anointing, together with the correct infrastructure, grows the church."

Then, an idea came into my head. In my mind, I began to see the problem of why people were not staying when they visited. We were failing to keep the back door closed. He was sending the people through the front door, but the back door was never closed. Five would come, and four would not come back. Ten would visit on a Sunday, and six would not return next Sunday. So, the numbers never increased because of that. The Holy Spirit gave me the plan of how to fix it. He gave me a four-pronged system that remedied the problem. The system went like this: First, the visitor would fill out a welcome card during the service when they first visited. Second, the day following their visit, my office would send out a card thanking them for worshipping with us. Third, two days later, my office would call the person on the phone to confirm that they received the card in the mail and to verbally thank them again for worshipping with us. Here, the person would be invited back for the next Sunday's service. Fourth, two days after that, my office would send another email to remind them of the upcoming Sunday service and how much we were looking forward to seeing them again. Week after week, our retention level started to increase. Not only were visitors coming, but they were coming back and staying. The church began to grow. As the Holy Spirit continued to move powerfully, people were being healed and delivered, and many testimonies started to come. People started watching our videos on social media and television. We had a program on the Word Network that started to give us a national and international platform. The anointing increased. The healings and deliverances were being watched by thousands and even millions around the world. People started to travel to Yonkers, New York, to our church that only held two hundred people. The crowds got so big that we didn't have room. They kept on coming. Sometimes, they were standing outside on the sidewalk in front of the church because there was no room inside the building. Those sick with different types of diseases and those who were bound by evil spirits filled the place every week. The infrastructure had met the anointing, and it caused an explosion of growth.

What a fabulous Helper and Counselor we have. When He guides you, know that you will arrive at your destination of success. When He tells you to do something, and you do it, know that you will never fail. The Holy Spirit, as the Senior Partner in your life, ministry, business, and family, will make you succeed beyond anything you could ever imagine. Oh, what a marvelous Friend He is. To know Him is to know the Best!

The Secret: Learn To Rest In Him

My friend, I want to tell you that I have found the secret of an abundant life here on earth. It is all found in embracing, knowing, and walking with the Holy Spirit. Before I met Him as a Person and a Friend, I was struggling in my Christian walk. I was praying and reading the Bible every day and going to church every week. But something was missing. In those days, I was "pushing" too hard and working too much, trying to win points with God. But the more I "tried," the more I failed. One day, I received a call from my spiritual father, Bishop Roy Bryant Sr., whom God used to introduce me to the Holy Spirit. He saw that I was struggling, trying my best to discharge the ministerial duties I had at the church. He said to me, "Son, you need to learn how to rest in the Holy Spirit."

I had no idea what that meant, and I said, "Bishop, what does that mean?" He was a man who had been walking with the Holy Spirit for over 50 years. He knew something that I needed to learn, and I needed to learn it fast before things got worse. For months, I pondered his statement. Little by little, I began to understand how to rest in the Holy Spirit. I began to stop trying so hard. I started to surrender all my cares of life and ministry to Him. With practice, I began to trust and surrender to Christ by Him. I started to find peace, and the burden of ministry started to disappear. Immediately, I started to notice that my anointing became stronger. My faith became more profound, and the results when I prayed for the sick and ministered deliverance to the demonized were more tangible. Praise the living God! When I learned to rest in Him, I really started resting.

CHAPTER 19

Knowing His Voice

"God, who at various times and in various ways spoke in time past to the fathers by the prophets, has in these last days spoken to us by His Son, whom He has appointed heir of all things, through whom also He made the worlds."
(Hebrews 1:1-2 NKJV)

God speaks to His children in a very tangible way. Because God is a Spirit, we must understand that He is not limited to communicating His thoughts in just one way or the way we, as human beings, think He should speak to us. Everything God does, He does it by His Spirit, including speaking to us. God's voice is heard from Spirit to spirit. But how do we get to know His voice? Let me tell you how I learned to hear and know His voice. As I spent time with the Holy Spirit alone in my prayer room, I started to learn how to quiet myself, my mind, and my thoughts and tune out all the noise of life sounding in my head and my body.

God created you and me to be able to communicate with Him very easily. It is beautiful, and a lot of His children forget. Let's take a journey to your place of birth as a human being. After He created everything, God looked at His creation and was not completely satisfied. How do I know? The Bible says that after

He finished creating the beast, cattle, and creeping things, He looked at it and said that it was "*good*."

> "*And God made the beast of the earth according to its kind, cattle according to its kind, and everything that creeps on the earth according to its kind. And God saw that it was good.*" (Genesis 1:25 NKJV)

Did you see that? But after creating man, He changes His expression and description of His next part of creation. The Bible gives us a hint that there was a difference between the other parts of creation and man. When He created man, He called it "indeed very good." Adding the word "indeed" to "very good" carries the idea of something that is without any question good, truly and undeniably. It is often used interjectionally to express surprise. In other words, when He created everything else, God was not surprised at what He saw, so it was "good." But when He created man in His image and likeness, He looked at the man, and the expression was, "Indeed, it was very good." God was surprised at how beautiful, unique, and different this creature was. Of course, He was looking at Himself. He didn't see the image of Himself when He looked at the dry ground, trees, fish of the sea, and birds of the air, but with the man, He saw Himself for the first time. It was this that made Him say, "Indeed, it was very good."

> "*Then God saw everything that He had made, and **indeed it was very good**. So the evening and the morning were the sixth day.*" (Genesis 1:31 NKJV)

Now, why did I explain all of that to you? Because to position yourself to hear God's voice, you must first know who you are in His eyes. Second, you must understand that God wants to communicate with Himself; that's you and me. His love for you is unimaginable. He longs to commune with you each day. To know His voice is the greatest point of relationship that you can have with the Holy Spirit. Jesus said,

> "My sheep hear My voice, and I know them, and they follow Me." (John 10:27 NKJV)

Here is the Key

To know His voice is to become familiar with Him. The Holy Spirit cannot lead us unless we know His voice. His voice is multifaceted. He speaks in different ways to us, and we must know it for us to follow Him. He can speak to you by an impression deep in your heart that gives you peace about making a certain decision. Peace in your heart is Him speaking to you to go ahead. Sometimes, a certain thought comes into your mind that lines up with His Word, His character, or His personality. That's His voice, too. But how you know His voice is connected to how much time you spend with Him. It is like this: I've been married to my wife Carol for over 35 years. But when I first met her, the first few times she called me, I had to really tune in to recognize her voice on the phone. The more we spent time together and conversed, the more I began to recognize the tone, the character, the pitch, and the sound of her voice on the phone when she called me. I no longer needed to ask the caller who was calling. I knew it was her because of the time we spent together. What made me want to spend time together with her? Desire! You must begin with the desire to know His voice. The key to getting to know His voice is to have the deep longing desire to know Him; otherwise, He will hide from you. That desire leads you to want to spend time with Him in fellowship, and the deeper the relationship you have with Him, the clearer His voice becomes to you.

Remember, you were made in the image of God. God wants to communicate with Himself. He wants to talk to you and through you. A desire to know His voice has been embedded into your makeup since He created you. When Adam was made alive, the first one he had an encounter with was with the Holy Spirit. The first one he saw was the Holy Spirit. The first one he spoke with was the Holy Spirit. The first one He walked with in the Garden of Eden was the Holy Spirit, because it was the Holy Spirit that gave him life. Since He was the one who gave you life, He wants to commune with you and for you to know His voice.

> "And the LORD God formed man of the dust of the ground, and breathed into his nostrils the breath of life; and man became a living being." (Genesis 2:7 NKJV)

To know His voice is to know life. When you get to know His voice, you really can get to know Him. The breath of God is the Holy Spirit. It was the same voice that spoke to Adam. It was the same voice that spoke to Moses and guided him throughout the wilderness passage to lead the people. It was the same voice that spoke to the children of Israel with thunder and lightning in the wilderness. It was the same voice that spoke out of the clouds when John baptized Jesus at the river Jordan. It was the same voice that spoke to the disciple at the Mount of Transfiguration, saying, "This is my beloved Son, in whom I am well pleased. Hear Him" (Matthew 17:5b NKJV). It was the voice of the Holy Spirit that they all heard and that is the voice you hear today. Do you know His voice? Have you ever heard His voice? I'm sure you have, even if you have not recognized it. But know that the voice that you hear is the voice of the Holy Spirit. People say, "God spoke to me." They are not wrong when they say that. But God the Father does not speak directly to man. He speaks by His Spirit. So, the voice that you hear speaking to your heart is the voice of the Holy Spirit. Oh, how glorious it is to know His voice.

CHAPTER 20

Recognizing When He Moves

(He Will Guide You)

Many of God's people today are in dire straits because they have not understood the importance of His Presence, which helps to recognize when He is moving. Have you ever been on a cruise ship? My wife and I love to cruise, and we have been on many of them on different occasions. On one occasion, I had the privilege of going to the bridge of the ship to see the captain and how he navigates. I was amazed at how a large vessel weighing over 200 tons and carrying over 4,000 passengers could be moved by such small equipment. The captain just sat in his captain's chair, and with a few pushes of different buttons and a joystick, he guided the big ship. I thought to myself, how can this be possible? I found out from the captain that what facilitated the ship's smooth movement was not only the sophisticated equipment, but it was also the water beneath the ship that allowed him to move the ship in any direction he wanted. He later explained that he knew that the ship was moving, not only by what he saw on the digital panel but by the mere "feeling" the ship was moving. His panel and his feeling told him that the ship was moving and in which direction.

Your Inner Navigation System

God has given you your own internal spiritual navigational system. It is called your spirit man. With your trained spirit, you can discern another spirit. Have you ever gone into a place and felt an unwelcome, evil presence there, or as if someone was watching you, but you never got to see anyone there physically? Of course you have. What you felt didn't come from your mind or your flesh; it came from your inner man, your spirit. Immediately, you knew something was not right. Well, God created a spirit in you to be able to communicate with the spirit world where He dwells. The Holy Spirit knows that, so He begins to do something, but He wants you to follow Him in what He's doing. His Presence needs to be picked up by your spirit, and when you do, then you can sense what He wants to do and which way He wants to go in your church service or in your life.

Many times, people ask me, "Ed, how do you know when the Holy Spirit is moving?" Here's what I say, "I spend time with Him, so I know." When you spend time with someone, you get to know them and almost anticipate what they're going to do next. You get to know their mind and thoughts, what bothers them, and what pleases them. As of the writing of this book, I have been married to my wife, Carol, for thirty-five years! It has been a wonderful life with her and our children. I thank God for blessing me with such a wonderful, virtuous woman. Because I've been married to my wife for so long, I know how she is going to react based on factors in the atmosphere, people around her, and the type of conversation that is taking place. I also know when she wants to talk, what she does not want to talk about, and when she wants to sit down or dance some more. (By the way, my wife and I like to dance with each other at home or the wedding of a friend or family member). To recognize when the Holy Spirit is moving, you sense it in the atmosphere. Sometimes, you feel led to something different than what you originally had in mind. At other times, you see how people are reacting to a certain worship song that is being sung by the worship team. Yet, at other times, you feel the anointing lifting from what you are doing at the moment. That means the Holy Spirit wants you to stop doing that and wait for His next instruction. The only way you can know is through knowing Him in the Secret Place. The more time you spend with Him, the more you will recognize when He's moving. And know this: when He moves, He moves like a wind. You cannot have a preconceived idea of how He should move or in which direction. Just like a wind that no one can predict its movement, so is the Holy Spirit. Remember, He is called the Spirit of Liberty (2 Corinthians 3:18).

All you need to do is follow His direction when He moves. Sometimes, before I begin to preach, I may hear a certain song resonating in my heart that I begin to sing. It could be the chorus to "How Great Thou Art," or "Holy Spirit, Thou Art Welcome in this Place." As I begin to sing, I begin to sense in my spirit what He wants to do in the service. Maybe He wants me to preach on a subject that I was not planning on that day. Or maybe He wants to speak a word of prophecy to someone who came to the service and who needs to hear from Him. He may want to begin to touch some of them with His healing and deliverance power. In any case, I must sense how He wants to move in the service and follow Him. The only way this can happen is if I know Him, and again, this happens when I spend time alone with Him. God has given you an inner navigational system; you can develop it by spending time with Him, and when you do, your ship will be moved as you sail upon His waters. Only don't sail against the current of the waters or the direction of the wind; allow the wind of the Spirit to take you so that you can get to your destination as you sail with Him. Trust me, you will not be disappointed!

CHAPTER 21

Ambassador of the Spirit

I am thankful, in a way that words cannot fully explain, for the Holy Spirit. He has taught me. He has led me. He has given me a purpose that goes far beyond the things that I have done to provide for my family. Better and bigger than any job that I have ever had is that which became heaven's mandate over me the moment I accepted what Jesus Christ accomplished on the Cross. It is the same mandate that the Father has declared over you if you have had a salvation experience.

The moment that you accepted Christ into your heart, you became a member of the Body of Christ and were deputized to carry out the will of God on Earth.

In the beginning, God not only created the heavens and the earth, He established an order and set humanity in place as the leader in creation. "Fill the earth and subdue it," God told Adam after He created him in the Garden of Eden. With this simple charge, God, who created all things, placed Adam in charge of all things on the earth. He handed him the authority to *lead, to rule, and to govern.*

Now, Under The New Covenant, That Mandate Doesn't Change

After Jesus was resurrected from the dead, He told his disciples, *"All authority has been given to Me in heaven and on earth. Go therefore and make disciples of all the nations, baptizing them in the name of the Father and of the Son and the Holy Spirit, teaching them to observe all things that I have commanded you."* (Matthew 28:18b-20a NKJV) Under the Old Covenant, God charged Adam to populate the Earth. Under the New Covenant, Jesus charges the disciples to populate the Kingdom! This population happens by occupying the nations of the earth and moving in the empowerment of the Holy Spirit to spread the culture of our Kingdom. This only happens when we live and move differently from the world even though we live in it.

In earthly governments, there is a designation called "Ambassador." An ambassador is *"an accredited diplomat sent by a country as its official representative to a foreign country."* Ambassadors are qualified. Ambassadors represent. Ambassadors are sent. Often, an ambassador sojourns to or is a temporary resident of the nation to which they've been sent.

This Is What We Are As Believers

> *"Beloved, I beg you as sojourners and pilgrims, abstain from fleshly lusts which war against the soul, having your conduct honorable among the Gentiles, that when they speak against you as evildoers, they may, by your good works which they observe, glorify God in the day of visitation."* (1 Peter 2:11-12 NKJV)

As believers in Jesus, we represent His Kingdom on Earth. No matter what nation you live in, your true home and your citizenship are in heaven. We are temples of the Holy Spirit and vessels that carry Him everywhere we go! Because of this, we ought to live according to the customs and laws of His Kingdom and not the kingdoms of this world. Like the scripture above suggests, and like an ambassador in government would be charged to do, we are to act in a way that honors the one we represent.

When the serpent deceived Eve into eating from the Tree of the Knowledge of Good and Evil, he convinced her to break the terms of her ambassadorship. By getting her to disobey God, he got her to break the connection with the source of her authority. She and Adam downgraded their positions from those of legislating ambassadors to something more closely related to foreign nationals. A foreign national is a person who lives in another country but is not a citizen. They have no special authority, no special rights, and no special privileges in the country in which they live. They do not represent their home country. The blood of Jesus did not only make atonement for our sins but restored us to our relationship with the Father. It also recommissioned us as deputies.

A deputy is *"a person whose immediate superior is a senior figure within an organization and who is empowered to act as a substitute for this superior."* Remember Matthew 28 when Jesus said that all authority was given to him? Well, Jesus also said, "*He who believes in Me, the works that I do he will do also; and greater works than these he will do*" (John 14:12 NKJV) and *"The Son can do nothing of Himself, but what He sees the Father do...For the Father loves the Son and shows*

Him all things that He Himself does...; For as the Father raises the dead and gives life to them, even so, the Son gives life to whom He will." (John 5:19-21 NKJV)

Reader, you have been sent into your generation, into your family, into your neighborhood with the mission of shining the light of Christ Jesus and making disciples of the people around you. The Holy Spirit has empowered you to do even greater works than Jesus did. You have all of the authority in the name of Jesus to do the will of God!

Go forth!

CHAPTER 22

From Washington Heights to the Ends of the Earth

When I first thought about writing this book, I thought back to my early days growing up in Washington Heights _ a small boy coming from a Latino Dominican family who was not rich, whose parents had minimal education, and who lived in a predominantly Dominican community. The community I come from is a hard-working community. Many have opened "bodegas" or grocery stores, and this is how many have been able to get above the poverty line. At the same time, in this community, many have turned to worshipping the occult because they think it promises them a better life and protection. This is a community where many never go to college or university, hence they wind up either in low-paying jobs or turning to the streets to make money from the sale of drugs. It was from here that God called me.

When I began my walk to know the Holy Spirit, I could have never imagined what would happen to my life and ministry so many years later. Through baseball, the hand of the Spirit brought me out, empowered me, anointed me, and put a word in my mouth to declare to the people of the world that Jesus Christ is Lord, a healer, a deliverer, and a Savior. Who would have thought I would wind up preaching the Gospel of Jesus Christ to numerous nations (and still counting)? Only the Holy Spirit can do this through a nobody who came from a simple family. Is there anything too hard for God? Absolutely nothing! God is able to do exceedingly, abundantly above anything we can ask or think (Ephesians 3:20).

I have found out the most exciting and most fabulous news anyone could have found. The Holy Spirit is the greatest gift given to man. People say, "No He is not; it is Jesus!" I often tell them to show me the difference between Jesus and the Holy Spirit. There is no difference. Jesus is here with us now, living inside of us by His Spirit. I want to shout from all the mountaintops of the world that the Holy Spirit is the key and answer to everything. The good news is that this promise is for all who will be willing to receive Him. The Bible makes an apparent fact about that. The Holy Spirit is available to all.

> *"And it shall come to pass in the last days, says God, that I will pour out of My Spirit on all flesh;*
> *Your sons and your daughters shall prophesy, your young men shall see visions, your old men shall dream dreams. And on My menservants and on My maidservants, I will pour out My Spirit in those days; and they shall prophesy."*
> (Acts 2:18-19 NKJV)

He was available to Jesus, Moses, Abraham, Isaac, Jacob, David, the prophets, and the Twelve Apostles, and He is available to you. We are living in days that are greater than the Book of Acts. Why? Because God wants to use you more now than then. The Bible says that where sin abounds, grace much more abounds (Romans 5:20). Therefore, there is a greater need for God's power to be extended to humanity. Look at the world governments. They are in shambles. They have no concrete answers for their nations' problems. Around the world, poverty, sickness, wars, and natural disasters are claiming millions of lives every year. Does God have an answer for all of this? Yes, of course.

Child of God, listen to me very well. God has made you to be a sign and a wonder to the people of this world. You were born for such a time as this. This generation is crying, and it needs you. God has heard their cries, and He has sent you to help answer the cries of millions. What is needed today more than ever is power. True power. The power of God is the only power that can bring immediate solutions to people. The Holy Spirit is the power that can transform lives and nations. The Holy Spirit doesn't just want to transform your life, He wants to partner with you to see the purpose and plan of God accomplished in the world today. When you yield to His voice and follow His leadership, the Holy Spirit can take you from obscurity to the limelight of God, from nothing to something and from beneath to above. You will go from your own "Washington Heights" of life to the ends of the earth all by His miracle-working power.

The church is the only organism on the earth that has been promised the Holy Spirit. Today, I believe that the time is coming when the church of Jesus Christ will be stronger than ever. It will be a church of power and a church triumphant. The harvest of the last days will be greater than in the days of the apostolic church in the Book of Acts. I see millions and billions turning to Christ's power rather than the devil's power. The Holy Spirit is raising an army that will be vested with power from above. An army who will preach the gospel with signs following like the world has never seen. In the middle of the street, there shall be healings, deliverance, and even resurrection from the dead. It will be a sign to this end-time generation of the coming of the Messiah. The only way this will be accomplished is as the church turns again to the one that raised Jesus from the dead — The Holy Spirit. May you become part of this army, and may you receive your marching orders to conquer the enemies of the cross, all through the power and grace of the Best Friend in the World—The Holy Spirit.

About the Author

Ed Citronnelli is the founder of World Healing International Church and Ed Citronnelli Ministries, which has multiple branches in New York, Ecuador, and Dallas, Texas, where it is headquartered. The church is multiracial and multicultural, with 24 different nationalities comprising the congregation. With a powerful healing, deliverance, miracle and prophetic ministry, Pastor Ed does the work of an evangelist and an apostle as he travels around the world preaching the Gospel of the Kingdom of God, with signs confirming his message. In his massive Holy Spirit Miracle Crusades, the deaf hear, the mute speak, the blind see, the crippled walk, and thousands come to the Lord Jesus Christ for the salvation of their souls. Since the time he began to know the Holy Spirit as a person, his life and ministry have never been the same. He testifies that the Holy Spirit has made the difference in everything he does. He is often found saying that the Holy Spirit is the key to his success, and in every gospel and miracle campaign, he openly asks the crowd to please welcome his Best Friend, the Holy Spirit.

He has been married to his beautiful wife Carol for 35 years, and the Lord has blessed them with three wonderful and God-fearing children: Justin, Gabrielle, and Hannah, and two grandchildren as of the writing of this book.

Milton Keynes UK
Ingram Content Group UK Ltd.
UKHW021336061224
3480UKWH00031B/122